Contents

Introduction

Histories are more full of examples of the fidelity of dogs than of friends.
    Alexander Pope.

The alliance of man and dogs goes back to at least the Stone Age. They probably first met as competitors in their search for food. The dog was the better hunter, man the more cunning. Man was able to take advantage of the dog's keener hearing to warn of enemies and of his scenting ability to help find and run down game. Meanwhile, the animal was fed, shared a warm abode, and gradually learned to accept a subservient role in the partnership. Thus, a great and lasting friendship was born.

In the heyday of Egyptian power, a ruler wouldn't be found dead without his dog. Amtefa II of the XI Dynasty and his Pharaoh Hound were entombed together, about 2,300 B.C. Socrates took an oath on the head of the *Canis familiaris.* Alexander the Great proclaimed, "If I were not a man I would like to be a dog." Napoleon would have missed his imperial return to Paris, had he not been rescued from drowning by a Newfoundland, as he was spirited off the island of Elba. When Vikings explored the North American waters, Norwegian Elkhounds were on the prows of their ships.

Dogs and People

The dog doesn't feel himself a pet but rather one of the family. No other animal has that strong affection for man. Fido cares less about other canines than he does about humans. A bitch doesn't remember her puppies a few months after they have been whelped but she remembers the children of her household. So people find in their pets a responsive, devoted friend. Youngsters especially relate to the animal, which frequently is used as an intermediary to reach the withdrawn child. The dog, too, fills a particular need for the elderly. In his loving, the dog doesn't care about age, beauty, or wealth.

Unlike so many pets, the dog has proved his utilitarian value. Centuries ago, when man began to domesticate other animals, the dog learned to round up flocks of sheep, to drive cattle, and to fight off predators. So when the Roman armies crossed the Alps and swept across Central Europe, to supply meat they brought along cattle. To move and guard the cattle were the Roman dogs. As the herds decreased, fewer dogs were needed, so they were left in some of the conquered countries. The Rottweiler is said to be a descendant of these cattle dogs.

Today, many German Shepherds and Doberman Pinschers have been trained as guard dogs to protect plants, stores, and individuals. Since 1952, Macy's department store in New York City has maintained a kennel of Dobermans to patrol the big building after it has been closed. Not only have the Dobes discovered after-hour thieves, but they have prevented damaging fire by smelling smoke and alerting their handlers.

The stories of St. Bernards working with the monks in the Swiss Alps are legion, the noble animals serving as pathfinders in the snow and locating persons overcome in the storms. In clear weather, a Saint has been known to scent a human more than 800 feet and they have found people buried under seven feet of snow. If the dogs could talk, they would be in demand as weather forecasters: as much as an hour before a snowstorm the dogs become restless.

Newfoundlands long have served as lifesavers. In 1919, a Newf named Tang swam ashore with a line from a ship sinking off Nova Scotia, helping to save the crew and passengers.

▲ Sled dog team on the trail ▼ Fox hunt in England

In police work, German Shepherds, Labrador Retrievers, Schnauzers, and Rottweilers have proved invaluable, patrolling the streets and helping to sniff out narcotics and explosives. In London, 280 of Scotland Yard's four-footed policemen guard the city and not a drug raid is carried out without the dogs. In Rome, a German Shepherd, called *Il Gigante* (The Giant) was on the books of the police department as a corporal. When the 140-pounder (64 kg) was retired in 1961, after 15 years on the force, he was credited with 400 arrests, more than any human Italian detective in that period.

When it comes to sheep, most of us are familiar only with the bedtime-counting variety. But in many lands, the woolly animals still are a basic source of income. So it is that the Collie and his little cousins, the Shetland Sheepdog and Border Collie, play key roles. Samoyeds pulled the sleds of Admiral Robert E. Peary as he discovered the North Pole in 1909. Two years later Samoyeds carried Roald Amundsen to the South Pole. For years German Shepherds, and Labrador and Golden retrievers have led the sightless.

Before You Buy

In owning a dog, you assume a great responsibility. Not only will you have to spend many hours training, feeding, and exercising the pup but you must be prepared to take the animal out at night and consider what you will do with the dog if you go away. A prospective owner also should consider the cost. There may be visits to the veterinarian, a boarding kennel, and with some breeds—poodles, terriers, and several of the sporting variety—frequent trips to grooming salons.

Then you must do some soul-searching. What type of dog would best fit your mode of life? How much time can you spend in training? Who will do the exercising? Does your family want a dog? Are the children old enough so they won't abuse the animal? If the children are the ones who are so anxious to have the pet, will they be willing to take care of it?

If you then decide to get the dog, what size, type, and sex do you want? Will it be long- or shorthaired, a purebred or a mutt? A purebred has been bred true to type for many generations.

You know its characteristics: its size, color, and potential as a

hunter, retriever, watchdog. The mongrel is a mixture and it is a gamble. The cuddly pup may grow to be a giant. Never buy a puppy on impulse, for the little ball of fur is the world's best salesman. You will spend many years with him.

Some people choose a dog to reproduce their own personality, others to complement or compensate for lack in their own image. Many want the *Canis familiaris* as a status symbol. But there are still others that simply want a responsive friend.

Terriers fit nicely into a home where there may be some rough-housing. Most of the toy breeds are too fragile for children. However, toys make excellent pets for the senior citizen since these little dogs can be paper-trained and require almost no exercising.

If you want a watchdog, it isn't necessary to have a giant animal. Any canine has sharp hearing and will bark an alarm. Although many of the larger dogs are quiet and easy to manage, obviously you will have space problems in a small apartment with a Great Dane, Newfoundland, or St. Bernard.

It doesn't really matter whether you buy a dog or bitch. Some people feel the bitch is the more affectionate, better with children, and easier to housebreak, but much depends on the individual animal and its training. Most males are more aggressive, have the urge to roam, and require more walking. The bitch, however, does come into season and must be **9**

▲ *Puppies for sale*

watched during the three weeks of heat. If you are not going to breed her, it is advisable to have her spayed. The idea that it will make her overweight or change her personality is false.

With coat, a longhaired dog requires grooming anywhere from daily to weekly. When he sheds, the hair comes out by the handful. Shorthaired smooth coats are much easier to care for, although the stiff hair is difficult to get out of furniture.

The prospective owner must decide whether to buy a young pup, an older one, or an adult. A pup never should be acquired until it is eight weeks old. Although you will have extra work the first few months, there is the pleasure of watching it grow. The older pup already has had its second and most important innoculations. He is stronger and easier to housebreak. The adult usually is housebroken, leash-trained, and has attained his full growth and true color.

Housebreaking

Almost all dogs can be trained but some are more intelligent and take to the work easier. However, on your part it is going to take patience, consistency, and kindness. If you give a pup an order, you must see it is obeyed.

But let us start at the beginning. The pup is brought into the house and being curious will want to sniff all the corners. He also should meet the members of the family. In his excitement, he probably will leave a few wet spots. Don't punish him at this stage. Just mop up.

There are two methods of housebreaking a puppy: taking him out at regular intervals or using papers. The first system of going outdoors is preferable because using the newspapers, he is encouraged to relieve himself in the house. A young puppy has little control, so minutes after eating he should be taken for a walk, and that means four times a day. In addition, he should go out the first thing in the morning, the last time before bed, and every time he awakens. The same route should be covered each time. He may find one place to go and if he does, take him to that spot each time. If there is a yard, he will find his own pet place. When he performs, praise him lavishly. Regularity is the key to success. A puppy will move three or four times a day and urinate ten to twelve. As he gets older, the pup gains better control and the walks can be reduced. He will go more readily if other dogs have been there before. If you can walk him with an older dog, it will help.

The paper system is employed by many apartment dwellers, and a thick Sunday paper is a big help. In a linoleum-covered room, spread newspapers over most of the floor and wait for the pup to use them. Remove the soiled papers and replace with fresh. After a couple of days reduce the area of the floor covered with papers. If you see the pup sniff or squat and he isn't on the paper, quickly place him on it. If you catch him in the act, sternly reprimand him. Before putting down fresh paper, as you keep reducing the protected area, always leave one sheet on which he has urinated as a reminder to the pup, for he probably will return to that spot. As the days go by, the bare space on the floor should increase until you are down to two newspaper sheets. During the training period, keep the pup confined to one room. When you begin to take him outside, you may have to place a newspaper on the curb.

You can make it a little easier for the pup if you avoid giving him water two hours before he goes to sleep. It is preferable to wait until the pup is three months old before housebreaking, when he has more control and understanding to cooperate. Don't be discouraged. It may take innumerable times before the pup gets the idea. When he performs always praise; scold when he fails. What is necessary is love and persistence. And as he gets to know you he learns to love and trust you, too. Remember, it takes *patience*.

Feeding

Although many people feed their dogs table scraps, frequently the scraps do not provide the balanced and complete nutrition he needs. It is better to use the commercial products, which come in three forms—dry, canned, and soft moist. Dry food is the most inexpensive and popular. It gives the dog an opportunity to exercise his gums and teeth and reduces tartar formation. It is produced by blending all the ingredients needed for a complete and total diet. It may be used dry or moistened with water or broth. Mixing a little specialty meat with dry food will enhance the palatability.

All dogs, from massive Great Danes to tiny Chihuahuas, need the same nutrient requirements. Only the amounts of food vary, and this is determined by the animal's age, activity, size, temperament, and living conditions. It is best to follow the directions suggested by the dog-food manufacturer on the label. However, be prepared to make adjustments if necessary. Don't forget to consider the shape of the animal's face and the length of his ears when choosing his feeding dish.

12 Regular feeding hours should be chosen. Puppies from

weaning to three months should have four meals a day, those from three to six months can have three meals, from six months to a year, two meals, and after a year old just one. A pup should be fed only enough to keep him strong and healthy. If he leaves food in his dish, the quantity should be reduced. A bowl of fresh water should be available at all times.

Fussy eaters usually are the fault of the owner, who gives tidbits from the table. The animal's food should always be put in his dish. If he doesn't eat, after a half-hour or so, remove the dish. Then give him his food at his next regular feeding. He won't starve. An overweight dog should have his daily intake of food reduced and he should be exercised more often. A dog shouldn't be fed before a long car trip or an air flight. If he's been playing hard, it is also advisable to let him relax a bit. When a pup is about four months old, a large bone, such as a beef knuckle or shank, is good to help him get rid of the baby teeth. It also helps to stop the urge to chew furniture. Sharp bones from poultry, chops, or fish must be avoided for they can splinter, damage the mouth, puncture the intestinal tract or stomach, or get lodged in the throat.

Two common fallacies are that garlic will prevent or cure worms and raw eggs will make the coat shiny. All garlic will do is make your dog socially inacceptable while raw egg white interferes with the absorption of biotin, a vitamin, and may cause diarrhea. Incidentally, diarrhea is the symptom of a number of disorders. If it should be only a slight occurrence, withhold food for awhile. But if it continues or if your dog is having digestive problems, consult your veterinarian. Next to yourself, he's your dog's best friend.

Obedience Training

To qualify as a pet, every dog should have some basic obedience training. Indeed, the difference between a trained and untrained dog is one letter, "s," for the former is a pet and the untrained a pest. A well-trained dog is happier and more welcome in the community.

A dog tires easily and so do you, so keep your training periods short, 10 to 15 minutes, or three 5-minute sessions. Most schools will not accept a pup for serious training until he **13** is six months old, although for simple obedience for the home, they will take him at four months. In preparation for his schooling, the dog should have a metal link training collar, or if he is a small animal, a nylon one. Be careful in the use of the collar for a constant pull on it could injure the pup. This is particularly true of toy breeds. A quick, light tug on the leash is sufficient to give the message. Then the pressure immediately should be released.

The first lesson is to have him walk beside you on your left. This is called heeling. Keep the leash short so the dog must stay close. It is better to start in a quiet secluded area, where there are no distractions. As you start walking say "Rover, heel." If he lags, give the lead a few quick jerks to get him alongside and repeat the command. When he does, praise him. Should he walk ahead of you, give him a "Rover, no," and pull him back in position. Remember, he learns by repetition. When you feel he is making progress, take him to the street. Always use the word "Heel." After a successful session, reward with a puppy biscuit. However, the best reward a dog receives is your praise. He wants to please you.

Next lesson is the "Sit." With the leash in your right hand, and the dog on your left side, give the order "Sit." At the same time, press down on his rump with your left hand while your right hand pulls his head up and in position with the leash. Then praise. Repeat the exercise and perhaps this time give him a puppy biscuit. Soon he will learn without your having to push his rump down. If he should lie down, get him up to the proper position, so he knows what you want.

After the sit comes the "Down." This can be done similarly as the sit, except you pull his front legs out from under him with the right hand.

The final command is "Come," and this can be the most difficult. Some trainers go to the room where the pup has been confined and call him by saying "Rover, come." His natural tendency is to run to you, especially if he has been alone for a few minutes. Each time you do it, repeat the word and praise him when he responds. Another method is to call the pup, "Rover, come," and pat the floor, your leg, or squeak a toy. If you call him and he doesn't respond, a light rope attached to

14

his collar can be used. If he resists, repeat the command, along with a few yanks. It may be necessary to haul him all the way. When he arrives, give him lavish praise.

Never work too long and don't train if you are tired. You must be firm when giving an order and the dog must obey. When he disobeys, scold him. Get him accustomed to one-word commands and always use the same —"No," "Heel," "Down," "Good," "Bad." The most important words in the dog's training lexicon are "No" and "OK."

The dog learns by associating what he does with the consequences of that behavior. If it is something that brings pleasure—praise, petting, or a snack—he is likely to repeat that behavior. Never call a dog to punish him—it only encourages him not to obey.

15

▲ Retrieving a dumbbell over a jump

Grooming

Shorted-coated breeds, like a Boxer or smooth Dachshund, need little grooming. A special glove with short, stiff bristles in the palm (sometimes called a hound glove) or a medium-soft brush can be used weekly to eliminate dead hair and to give the coat a gloss. Loose hair left on the coat surface should be wiped off with a soft cloth. When brushing or combing, it is advisable to start with the dog's hindquarters—he won't object as much to what he can't see.

Long-coated dogs come in three categories: double coat, medium, and heavy. The double, consisting of long, coarse hair over a soft, dense undercoat, should be brushed daily. With a stiff long-bristled brush, begin from the skin out taking a small section of hair and pulling the brush or comb toward you. For the medium length coat, a firm bristle brush will do the job. The coat should be worked with the grain, giving special attention to the feathering. Any mats or tangles can be combed out gently or worked loose with your fingers, using a drop or two of oil. If the mat is impossible to get out, hold it in one hand, gently pulling the mat from the body, and snip it off along the grain of hair with a blunt-ended scissors. Tar, paint, or chewing gum can be softened with nail-polish remover.

Certain breeds require special trimming. Terriers who are

16

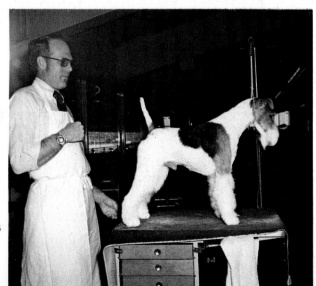

being shown need plucking, whereas clippers are used for housepets. The undercoat of the wirehaired variety should be removed at least once every six months, otherwise the owner will have a shaggy dog that scarcely resembles the breed. Poodle coats are dense and will mat if not groomed. It is advisable to go to a professional groomer.

Shedding is a normal procedure by which the dog gets rid of dead hair and grows a new coat. Usually it takes place early in the summer, but many dogs living in overheated apartments shed lightly all year long. If you do a good job of brushing, there will be little hair around the house.

When grooming your dog, you should be on the lookout for fleas, ticks, lice, or skin disorders. In using any of the effective insect powders, shampoos, dips, and sprays, be sure to avoid the dog's eyes. A tick buries its head in the skin, sucking the blood and swelling in size. Care must be exercised in removing it, for the head may remain inside and cause an infection. Dab the tick and skin with a piece of cotton soaked in oil or rubbing alcohol, and with broad-tipped tweezers gently pull the tick out. Put the tick in a cup of kerosene, turpentine, or alcohol or in a tissue and flush it down the toilet. Flea collars are effective against those ubiquitous pests, but must be replaced periodically. Some dogs are allergic to the collars.

You should examine your pet's nails, too. A housedog who spends much of his time on rugs isn't going to wear his nails down sufficiently and from time to time they will have to be trimmed with special clippers. If you do it, be careful not to cut the quick, for it is sensitive and will bleed. After clipping, file the rough edges. Some owners, fearful they may hurt the dog with clippers or scissors, only use a file.

Bathing

For the housedog, a good rule to follow is not to bathe him unless absolutely necessary. The bath washes out the natural oils and some of the dog soaps are irritating to his skin. Regular brushing and commercial dry shampoos should keep your dog presentable. However, if he has rolled in mud or something worse, there comes a time when he must take the plunge.

If possible, it is best to brush and comb him before a bath, for **17** tangles or mats are much harder to work out when the hair is wet. Have everything ready before you start: shampoo (preferably tearless), a bristle brush, a sponge, and a towel. A rubber mat will prevent him from slipping, and you may want to wear a plastic apron. Use lukewarm water and be certain it's not too hot. If you use a tub, fill it to his hips—most dogs don't like standing in too much water. A hand sprayer, which attaches to the faucet, makes the job considerably easier and you will not have to use a tub filled with water. With the hand sprayer, soak the dog thoroughly, if necessary forcing the water through the hair to the skin. Be careful not to get water in his eyes or ears. Next take a sponge saturated in the soap (if it is concentrated, dilute it in a separate dish) and work up a good lather. Use the small brush to get the lather over the entire body. Then rinse the dog thoroughly to get rid of all the soap. With a longhaired dog, gently squeeze and pat off the excess water and rub him briskly with a towel. An electric hair dryer will do a much better and quicker job, if your dog will submit. When he is completely dry, brush and comb him.

Dog Shows

Improvement of the breeds is the primary purpose of the dog show, but the lure of winning attracts fanciers all over the world to competition. Every weekend thousands take to the road, bound for show or field grounds. Some bring home ribbons, others more fortunate win trophies or cash prizes. But the vast majority gain little more than the fresh air and a pleasant day in the country. Although the tangible results are negligible, there is the satisfaction for the dog owner in proving "My dog is better than yours."

How does a judge make his or her decision? Each breed has a standard of perfection, and the arbiter strives to make a selection on a basis of that standard, choosing dogs he or she feels is closest to what would be the perfect dog for the breed.

Both men and women exhibit their pets and serve as judges. Age is no barrier. In one ring you are likely to see a teenager with her dog, while next to her is a senior citizen putting his pride and joy through its paces. If you've always dreamed of a stage career, here's a chance to perform. And if you get last-

minute jitters, it is always possible to have a professional
handler take Lassie into the ring, for a fee.

Be prepared to keep some unusual hours—most shows start
at 9 A.M. Some of the indoor events last into the night. Unlike
other sports activities, shows are never called off because of
inclement weather, so you may be exhibiting in rain or hail.

No movie star is beautified more than an Afghan or Poodle.
From the bath the night before until showtime, it takes at least
five hours to prepare the canine primadonna. After the oils and
lotions comes a session with brushes and combs, a manicure,
plastic curlers on the ears, topped off with hair spray so not a
hair is out of line. Then comes a downpour and our perfectly
groomed canine is just another naked pooch.

However, few events have the appeal of an outdoor show
when the air is crisp and there is bright sunlight. At the dog
show you are away from everyday cares. Once you have
joined the weekly parade to the grounds, you will meet many
people and make new friends. There is an international
cameraderie among dog owners, with an increasing number
attending or exhibiting around the world. **19**

▲ *A class being judged*

Field Trials

Every weekend throughout the year, sportsmen run their dogs in field competition. This consists of trials for pointing breeds, spaniels, retrievers, and hounds. Unlike showdog events, where there are prescribed standards for the judges, who are largely professionals, the field dogs work in wide open spaces and the arbiters are experienced amateurs. They are dedicated men and women who spend long hours on foot or horseback, following the dogs and evaluating their performances.

The pointing breeds—Pointers, Setters, German Short-haired and Wirehaired Pointers, Brittany Spaniels, Viszlas, Weimaraners, and Wirehaired Pointing Griffons—run in pairs (braces) in what are called heats. There is a set time for each heat, from a half-hour to three hours, and the dogs are judged on their style of running, use of wind and terrain in locating game, accurate nose, intensity on point, and keen desire to hunt. A dog must respond to his owner but he also is judged on his independent judgment in hunting a course.

The pointing dogs are particularly fast and will run out of gun range. When they locate birds they go into an immovable point and wait for the hunter. The dogs are followed by two judges who for better mobility and observation ride horses.

In spaniel trials, the English Springer, Cocker, and American Water stay within gun range, so the judges follow on foot. The dogs flush and retrieve the birds. The spaniels also have a water test but land work is the primary function. The dogs are judged for their game-finding ability, steadiness (see Glossary) to wing, shot, and command, and their retrieving ability. They must have soft mouths in handling the game. The dogs are sent off in braces, and there is no time limit in the heats.

The retrievers—Labradors, Goldens, Chesapeakes, Curly- and Flat-coated, and Irish Water Spaniels—work singly and must demonstrate their ability to retrieve with equal proficiency both on land and in water. A dog is judged on his natural abilities—memory, intelligence, attention, nose, courage, perseverance, and style — and on acquired talents — steadiness, control, response to directions, and delivery of the **20** bird. A dog is eliminated for a hard mouth (badly damaging

Hound trials are held for Beagles, Bassets, Dachshunds, Foxhounds, and the treeing breeds. The Beagle is acknowledged to be supreme in hunting the rabbit or hare. Beagles compete in braces and in small and large packs. Essentially a trailing hound, the Beagle's purpose is to find game, pursue it in an energetic and decisive manner, and to show a willingness to stay with it. He must be endowed with a keen nose, intelligence, and have an intense desire to hunt. Speed isn't as important as accuracy in trailing. In pack events, the team performance counts. Should a dog or two do most of the work, it is not considered a good pack.

The Basset's short legs enable him to keep his nose close to the trail without losing stride. So although he's slower than the other hounds, he's second only to the Beagle with rabbits. The same rules apply at Basset trials as at Beagle, with braces, and small and large packs.

In Dachshund events, the badger dogs are judged for their good noses, courage in facing punishing cover, keenness, perseverance, obedience, and ability to go to earth. Should a rabbit lodge in any earth or run through a drain large enough for a Dachshund to enter, the dog is expected to move in without hesitation.

All-age stakes at Foxhound trials last four days, with the hounds sent away at dawn, running until noon. They are judged for their hunting, trailing, speed, endurance, and drive. **21**

▲ *The "breakaway" of a heat at a field trial*

▲ Golden Retriever with pheasant ▲ Springer Spaniel flushes bird

1
Sporting

The sporting breeds fall into four categories: pointers, retrievers, setters, and spaniels. They have been bred for hunting, the pointers and setters going into their picturesque immovable stance to indicate the presence and position of a bird. The spaniels, smaller in stature, drive the birds from cover and cause them to take flight so the sportsman may take a shot. This is known as flushing a bird. The retriever recovers birds after they have been shot, either on land or over water. All of these dogs are known for their keen sense of smell and soft mouths for carrying birds. Conservationists hail their work in retrieving birds that have been shot and otherwise would be lost. The sporting dogs, strikingly beautiful with an air of nobility, generally are of good temperament and make excellent family and companion dogs. However, they like to run and require a good deal of exercise.

23

◀ *Brittany Spaniel on point
   while brace-mate waits*

Griffon, Wirehaired Pointing

Height, 19½–23½ inches (50–60 cm); weight, 50–60 pounds (23–27 kg).

Although the origin of the Wirehaired Pointing Griffon is Dutch, it is generally regarded as a French breed since much of its development was accomplished in France. E. K. Korthals began his breeding program in Schooten, Holland, but left for Germany, where he continued his work. There the dog is known as a Korthals Griffon. He also traveled to France, and the breed made great progress in both countries. Korthals wanted an all-purpose, close-working hunting dog that could be both a hunter and a retriever. Although the Griffon is a bit highstrung, he is gentle and obedient. This medium-sized dog has a fairly short back and is strongly limbed. Everything about him indicates strength and vigor. The coat is hard, dry, never curly, with a downy undercoat. His long head is covered with a harsh hair that forms a mustache and eyebrows. In color, the Griffon is steel gray or gray-white with chestnut splashes.

Editor's note: *The low range of the height and weight given for each breed is the minimum for bitches; the upper range is the maximum for dogs.*

Pointer

Height, 23–28 inches (58–71 cm); weight, 45–75 pounds (20–34 kg).

The Pointer is a picturesque dog. Bred primarily for sport afield, he should unmistakably look and act the part. The ideal Pointer gives the immediate impression of compact power and agile grace. The head, which is the hallmark of the breed, is noble and proudly carried. The muscular body bespeaks both staying power and dash. Here is an animal whose every movement shows him to be a hard-driving hunting dog, possessing stamina and courage. He is named for his mission in life—to point—and year after year he wins the majority of the field trial championships. The dark, round eyes (the darker the better) are bright, kindly, and intelligent. In color, the Pointer is liver, lemon, black, orange with white, or solid orange. The short coat is dense and smooth with a sheen. When he moves, the gait is smooth, the head carried high, the nostrils wide, and the tail moves from rhythmically side to side with the pace. Balance and overall symmetry are more important than size. The pointer's even temperament and alert good sense make him a congenial companion in the field and at home. In his expression is the loyalty and devotion of a true friend of man.

Pointer, German Shorthaired
and German Wirehaired

*Shorthaired: height, 21–25 inches (53–63 cm); weight,
45–70 pounds (20–32 kg). Wirehaired: height, 22–26 inches (56–66 cm);
weight, 50–75 pounds (23–34 kg).*

The Shorthaired Pointer is an all-purpose dog. He is a good
upland hunter with a keen nose, and is an excellent swimmer
for waterfowl work. The breed has quickly become popular in
the show ring, the field, and as a pet. The overall picture is that
of an aristocratic, well-balanced, symmetrical animal, with
conformation indicating power, endurance, and agility. There
is grace of outline, clean-cut head, sloping shoulders, deep
breast, powerful back, a well-carried docked tail. The skin is
close and tight, with the hair short, thick, and tough to the
hand. In color, he is liver and white spotted or ticked, solid
liver, and roan. He is gentle, learns quickly, and likes to roam.

The Wirehaired Pointer has been called "a shorthaired who
needs a shave." The coat is weather-resistant and to some
extent water-repellent. The undercoat is dense enough in
winter to insulate against the cold but thin in summer. The
distinctive outer coat is straight, harsh, and rather flat-lying.
From 1½ to 2 inches long, it does not hide the outline of the
body. It protects against rough cover in the field: the bushy
eyebrows, short beard, and whiskers guard the face from brush
and briars. Color is the same as the Shorthaired. The Wire is of
sturdy build, lively manner, and is rather aloof but not un-
friendly. He will protect the household but he is rather restless
for a city dog.

27

◀ *German Shorthaired* ▲ *German Wirehaired*

Retriever, Chesapeake Bay

Height: 21–26 inches (53–66 cm); weight: 55–75 pounds (25–34 kg).

This ''made-in-America'' breed had its start in 1807, when two puppies were rescued from an English brig that was wrecked off the coast of Maryland. The Chesapeake evolved after breeding with local hunting dogs. The Chessie was developed for his utilitarian value rather than his looks. He is an amazing water dog, and is a favorite of the duck and goose hunter. Big, tough, and rugged, he will plunge into icy waters and swim back with the bird. In color, he varies from dark brown to faded tan. Coat is extremely important since the dog is used for hunting in adverse weather conditions. The oil in the harsh outer coat and woolly undercoat prevents cold water from reaching the skin—the Chessie's coat resists the water the same way a duck's feathers do. When he emerges and shakes himself, his coat does not hold the water at all, being merely moist. This courageous workman will guard his family zealously; he is especially good with children. The Chesapeake has a mind of his own and he is apt to be a bit stubborn.

Retriever, Curly-coated and Flat-coated

Curly: height, 23–25 inches (58–63 cm); weight, 60–70 pounds (27–32 kg). Flat: height, 22–24 inches (56–61 cm); weight, 60–70 pounds (27–32 kg).

The least popular of the retrievers in this country is the Curly-coat. Why is hard to say, because he is devoted, learns quickly, and his coat requires very little trimming. He is an upstanding dog that has much endurance. His thick coat comes in good stead for his water work, at which he excels. Regardless of icy conditions, he will dive again and again to get his bird. The black or liver coat, a mass of curls all over, also protects against briars and brambles when he is hunting in heavy cover. The Curly-coat's head is well-proportioned, with jaws long and strong. He has rather large black or brown eyes. Smallish, low-set ears lie close to the head and are covered with curls. He is a good family dog, particularly with kids.

The Flat-coat at the turn of the century was the most popular dual-purpose dog in Britain. But in the United States it has never done well, which is surprising since he is such a splendid dog. Of medium size, he is a good worker on both land and water, and he likes everyone. The black or liver coat is dense, of fine quality and texture, and lies as flat as possible. The long head is nicely molded; the jaws are strong enough to carry a hare or pheasant. The brown or hazel eyes have a keen look. **29**

▲ *Flat-coated Retriever*

Retriever, Golden

Height: 21½–24 inches (54–61 cm); weight: 60–75 pounds (27–34 kg).

This is the glamour boy of the retrievers. With his lustrous golden coat he invariably commands attention. He is affectionate, easy-going, and eager to please. Because he learns quickly and is obedient, the Golden does well in the breed ring, in obedience trials, and as a guide dog for the sightless. He also makes a fine family pet.

The Golden is not as good a water dog as some of the other breeds, and his long coat may be a problem where there are burrs. He is a powerful, active dog, sound and well-put-together. He has a kindly, intelligent expression and has an air of self-confidence. In hunting, the Golden has a good nose and in retrieving a tender mouth. The brown eyes are set well apart and the ears are rather short, hanging flat against the head with rounded tips slightly below the jaw. The dense, water-repellent coat has a good undercoat and may be either straight or wavy. The texture of the hair is not as hard as that of a **30** short-coated dog nor as silky as a setter's.

Retriever, Labrador

Height: 21½–24½ inches (54–62 cm); weight: 55–75 pounds (25–34 kg).

The king of the retrievers is the Lab. He leads in number of registrations, wins many field trials, excels in the breed ring, does well in obedience events, guides the blind, and is used by police to smell out narcotics and explosives. Despite his name, he didn't come from Labrador but from Newfoundland. However, the breed was developed in England by the Earl of Malmesbury. For hunting, the Lab has a wonderful nose. He will trail a crippled bird great distances and still bring it to bag. A swift swimmer, he will plunge into the water and retrieve a duck. Upland, the Lab works like a spaniel, flushing grouse and pheasants. The Labrador is a strongly built dog. The coat is close, dense, straight, and gives a fairly hard feeling to the hand. In color, the Lab is black, chocolate, or yellow, which varies from fox red to light cream. A feature of the breed is the "otter" tail, which is broad at the base and tapers to a point. It is used as a rudder and for balance in the water. The Lab likes children and he will play with them around the fireplace one day and the next be retrieving in freezing weather. He is happy carrying a duck, pheasant, the morning paper, or a dumbbell, and he does it all with an air of joy and pride.

Setter,
English, Gordon, and Irish

English: height, 24–25 inches (61–65 cm); weight, 60–70 pounds (27–32 kg).
Gordon: height, 23–27 inches (58–68 cm); weight, 45–80 pounds (20–36 kg).
Irish: height, 25–27 inches (63–68 cm); weight, 60–70 pounds (27–32 kg).

The English Setter, one of America's top bird dogs, is blessed with a gentle, loving disposition that makes him also a perfect pet. Added to that, he is a strikingly beautiful dog who comes in a variety of colors—black, black and white, tan and white, orange or lemon and white, liver and white, or solid white. The setter makes an attractive picture in the field, with his head lifted high and his lustrous coat flowing in the breeze.

The Gordon Setter gets his name from the fourth Duke of Gordon in Scotland in the late 18th century. A black dog with

English ▲ Gordon ▼ Irish ▶

tan markings (either of rich chestnut or mahogany), the Gordon is a slow, methodical worker in the field. He has a good nose. His sturdy build suggests strength and stamina rather than speed. He is well muscled, with plenty of bone and substance, and his gait is bold and free-swinging. However, he is inclined to be a one-man or one-family dog.

The Irish Setter, with his flowing mahogany or chestnut red coat, is one of the most striking dogs in the show ring and invariably draws cheers. Most popular of the setters, his build is substantial yet elegant. At the trot his gait is big, lively, graceful, and efficient, with his head held high. He has a rollicking personality. The Irish is gentle with everyone but he must be watched for he loves to roam.

Spaniel, American Cocker

Height: 13½–15½ inches (35–40 cm); weight: 25–27 pounds (11–12 kg).

This is not only the smallest of the spaniels but the smallest of the sporting breeds. It was the nation's most popular dog in registrations from 1946 through 1952. The name is believed to have originated from the little spaniel's proficiency in hunting the woodcock. The Cocker still can work in the field if he is trained. However, in recent years, he has become so popular as a pet, his only hunting is trying to locate a puppy biscuit. The Cocker comes in three varieties: black, any solid color other than black (known as ascob), and parti-color (when two or more colors appear in clearly defined markings). The Cocker has a sturdy, compact body and cleanly chiseled and refined head, with the overall dog in complete balance. The official standard calls for the Cocker to be ''free and merry, well balanced throughout, and in action to show a keen inclination to work, equable in temperament, with no suggestion of timidity.'' The Cocker likes his home and family and adapts quickly to a surburban house or a city apartment. Intelligent, he is a fast learner. Grooming is required to keep the long flowing coat from matting. He likes to eat and will be overweight unless his owner refrains from feeding him all he asks for.

Spaniel, American Water

Height: 15–18 inches (38–46 cm); weight: 25–45 pounds (11–20 kg).

This is another of the four native North American breeds. Although he has been used extensively in the Midwest, the dog is fairly uncommon in other sections of the country. A dark liver or chocolate in color, this little spaniel only has been recognized by the A.K.C. since 1940. He is a working gun dog and is adept in flushing game upland or retrieving waterfowl. Not particularly handsome, he has a closely curled coat, developed to protect him against weather, water, or punishing cover. His head is moderate in length. The forehead is covered with short smooth hair, without a tuft or topknot. A medium-length muzzle is square. The long and wide ears are set not too high on the head, just slightly above the eye line. The tail, moderate in length, is covered with hair. He barks a bit more and is a little sharper in temperament than the other spaniels, but he is a good watchdog, and although restless, a quick learner.

35

Spaniel, Brittany

Height: 17½–20½ inches (45–52 cm); weight, 30–40 pounds (14–18 kg).

The Britt is a dog of paradoxes. He is a spaniel but he looks like a small setter. He is the only member of the spaniel family that does not flush his game—he points it. He is an excellent upland hunter and he retrieves as well. The French Brittany Club called him "a maximum of quality in a minimum of size." From the start, Brittany owners in the United States (the first Britts were not brought over until the 1930s) were more interested in working their dogs in the field than showing them. So today, many Britts are owned by one-dog sportsmen who are quite content to spend their weekends hunting. Ruggedness without clumsiness is a characteristic of the breed. A compact, closely-knit dog, the Britt is so leggy that his height at the shoulders is the same as the length of his body. The dog frequently is born tailless. If there is a tail it should not be more than four inches (10 cm) long. In color, the Britt is dark orange and white or liver and white. Some ticking is desirable in the coat. The hair is dense, flat or wavy, never curly or silky. It is not as fine as in other spaniel breeds. The Britt is very affectionate and likes everyone.

Spaniel, Clumber

Height: 16–19 inches (41–48 cm); weight: 35–65 pounds (16–29 kg).

The heaviest of the spaniel family is the dog named after Clumber Park, which was the estate of the Duke of Newcastle. The dogs were sent to the Briton by the Duc de Noailles, who had been breeding them in France. The Clumber was a great favorite of British royalty: Prince Albert, King Edward VII, and King George V all shot over him. A heavy, massive dog, he has a thoughtful appearance. The head is large and flat on top with a furrow running from between the eyes upon the center. The large hazel deep-set eyes have a dignified and intelligent expression. The ears are long and broad at the top and lie close to the head. The silky, straight coat is not too long but is quite dense. In color, the Clumber is white with lemon or orange markings, the fewer markings on the body, the better. The tail is docked. He is an easy-going, gentle dog. The Clumber likes to eat and unless he gets enough exercise will put on weight. **37**

Spaniel, English Cocker

Height: 15–17 inches (38–43 cm); weight: 26–34 pounds (12–15 kg).

The English Cocker is an attractive, active, merry little sporting dog, with a short body and strong legs. His movements are lively, his gait powerful and frictionless. He is always alert. While at work, the carriage of his head and his ever-wagging tail give the impression that here is a dog that is not only bred for hunting, but really enjoys it. He is strongly built and capable of top speed and great stamina. The English Cocker comes in a variety of attractive colors: black, red, liver, golden, black and tan, and tricolor. The roans come in blue, liver, red, orange, and lemon. The medium-length coat is flat or slightly wavy, and silky in texture. On the head, it is short and fine. There is sufficient undercoating to give protection in the field. The coat must be brushed and combed regularly to avoid matting. Some trimming is also required. The English Cocker craves companionship and makes a fine pet. He likes to eat, so don't fall for those pleading eyes and come up with extra **38** goodies or he will lose that good figure.

Field Spaniel ▶

Spaniel, Field and Sussex

Field: height, 18 inches (46 cm); weight, 35–50 pounds (16–23 kg).
Sussex: height, 15 inches (38 cm); weight, 35–45 pounds (16–20 kg).

Two of the rarest breeds in the world are the Field and Sussex spaniels. In 1967, when three Fields were registered with the A.K.C., none had been recorded in 26 years and only seven since 1929. He is lower slung than a Cocker. Black, liver, red, or tan, the coat is flat or slightly waved, and never curly. It is silky in texture, glossy and sufficiently dense to resist the weather. The Field's head, his outstanding characteristic, should convey the impression of high breeding and nobility. He has an even disposition: those who own the Field say he fits into the household very nicely.

From 1961 to 1969 only three Sussex were registered by the A.K.C. The rich golden color, which is a highlight of the breed, also has created problems. Some sportsmen claim it is difficult to see the Sussex when hunting, because his golden coat blends with the land. The dog's long, wide head is carried not much above the level of the back. His abundant coat is flat or slightly waved. The tail is docked. His short legs have heavy bones. The Sussex is not a particularly fast dog but he trains well and is a willing worker. He is inclined to howl a bit, and when hunting he gives tongue.

Spaniel, Irish Water

Height 21–24 inches (53–61 cm); weight: 45–64 pounds (20–29 kg).

The clown of the spaniel family, the Irish Water is also the tallest. The forte of this dog from Ireland is water work. He is a favorite dog of the duck hunter because he is a strong swimmer. The liver-colored dog also is proficient upland, for he has a good nose. His most striking features are his coat, where the back, neck, and sides are covered with tight, crisp ringlets; his topknot, consisting of long, loose curls that form a well-defined widow's peak between the eyes; and his "rat" tail, which at the root is thick and covered for two or three inches with short curls, and tapers at the end. The head is cleanly chiseled not cheeky. The long, lobular ears are abundantly covered with curls. The Irish sheds less than any of the other spaniels. He learns quickly but he is inclined to be headstrong.

Springer Spaniel, English and Welsh

English: height, 19–20 inches (48–51 cm); weight, 44–55 pounds (20–25 kg).
Welsh: height, 17 inches (43 cm); weight, 40 pounds (18 kg).

The English Springer is a medium-sized dog with a neat, compact body and a docked tail. He is a well-proportioned dog, and his muscular legs have enough length to carry him with ease. Taken as a whole, the Springer looks the part of a dog who can go and keep going under difficult hunting conditions and still enjoy what he is doing. The head is impressive without being heavy. His moderately long, glossy coat usually is liver and white or black and white, with feathering on the legs, ears, and chest. The coat is flat or wavy and dense enough to be waterproof, weatherproof, thornproof. More than any other feature, the eyes contribute to the Springer's appeal. The expression is alert, trusting, kindly. He is a fine family dog, easy to train, and exceptionally good with youngsters.

The Welsh is larger and stronger than the Cocker Spaniel but smaller than the English Springer. He is compact, built for endurance and activity. The Welsh likes to work in the field, has an excellent nose, and he does well in the water. A dark rich red and white in color, the Welsh has a coat that is flat, thick, and silky. He is easy-going but not as demonstrative as the English. He is a good watchdog.

▲ *Irish Water Spaniel* ▼ *English Springer Spaniel*

Vizsla

Height: 21–24 inches (53–61 cm); weight: 40–50 pounds (18–23 kg).

The Vizsla, added to the A.K.C. ranks in 1960, is also known as the Hungarian Pointer. He is a medium-sized hunting dog of distinguished appearance. He fills the need for the one-dog owner who desires both a family pet and a hunting companion. Robust but rather lightly built, his short coat is an attractive rusty gold. The Vizsla, one of the smallest of the all-round pointer-retriever breeds, is the national dog of Hungary. After surviving numerous wars over the centuries, the breed suffered a decline in the late 19th century that continued into the 20th. By the end of World War I the Vizsla was close to extinction, with only about a dozen of the true type left in Hungary. From that minimum stock, sportsmen nurtured the breed back again. The Vizsla has the temperament of the natural hunter. He is endowed with a good nose and above-average ability to take training. He is lively, gentle-mannered, and demonstratively affectionate. Obedient, fearless, with a well-developed protective instinct, the Vizsla wants to please. With his smooth coat, he needs very little grooming.

Weimaraner

Height: 22–28 inches (56–71 cm); weight: 55–70 pounds (25–32 kg).

The breed whose name comes from Weimar, the city of Goethe, was promoted by court nobility who wanted a dog for all-round hunting. Various crosses were tried with the Leithund being the basic breed. Later a German Weimaraner Association with very strict regulations was organized. To own a "gray ghost" one had to become a member of the club. When the breed was brought to America, there was a great ballyhoo about the Weimaraner being the top hunting dog of all time. When he was beaten in field trials, the advance propaganda backfired. The breed has gradually made a comeback and is now used more for hunting than in field trials. He is full of drive when working. The gray dog is fearless and very protective to his master and family. With his short, smooth, sleek coat, ranging in color from dark to silver gray, the Weimaraner is a picture of grace and alertness. He likes to run and requires plenty of exercise.

▲ *Greyhound racing* ▼ *Pack of hounds on the way to the hunt*

2

Hounds

The hounds can be separated into two divisions: sight and scent. Except that both types are hunters, there is little similarity between them in their body structure, in how they are used, or in their hunting. Scent hounds are more closely allied to the sporting breeds for they trail their game using their exceptional olfactory senses. They are said to have a good "nose," with the Bloodhound being number one in this category. Black and Tan Coonhounds, Bassets, and Otterhounds have musical, bell-like voices when they are on the trail, and Beagles and Foxhounds also give tongue on the chase. Afghans, Borzois, Salukis, and Greyhounds are typical of the sight variety. Possessed of keen eyesight and exceptional speed, they can locate, run down, and hold their quarry at bay until the hunter arrives. Most of the hounds should have plenty of room to run.

Afghan

Height: 25–27 inches (63–68 cm); weight: 50–60 pounds (23–27 kg).

The Afghan is an aristocrat, his whole appearance one of dignity and aloofness. He is often referred to as a king of dogs because of his regal bearing. His history has been traced back to between 4,000 and 3,000 B.C. The striking characteristics of the breed are an exotic "Eastern" expression; a long, silky topknot; prominent hipbones, higher and wider than in other dogs; profuse feathering on the legs; and a long, flowing coat. In Afghanistan, where the breed originated, there were two types of Afghans: those living in desert areas who did more running and had longer bodies; and those from the mountains, with a shorter back and hind legs, permitting more spring in the rocky terrain. All colors are permissible. The Afghan requires considerable brushing to prevent the coat from matting. Although easy-going, he is inclined to be independent and often is hard to housebreak. He never fails to draw admiring glances when he is walked on a city street.

Basenji

Height: 16–17 inches (41–43 cm); weight: 22–24 pounds (10–11 kg).

The barkless dog, as the Basenji is known, is depicted in Egyptian engravings in tombs of 3,600 B.C. But the breed faded into complete obscurity until 1870, when explorers in Central Africa came upon these dogs. It was not until 1937 when the dogs were at Crufts show in London that they finally attracted much attention—in fact so much so that special police had to move crowds past the Basenji benches. The Basenji is a small, lightly built, short-backed dog, giving the impression of being high on the leg compared to his length. The wrinkled head is proudly carried, and the dog's whole demeanor is one of poise and alertness. In color, the Basenji is chestnut red, pure black, or black and tan. The silky coat is short. The tail is on top and curled tightly over to either side. Although he does not bark, he makes noise described as a mixture between a chortle and a yodel. Basenjis are extremely clean dogs, some washing themselves like cats. This intelligent little dog from the Congo is somewhat stubborn and is a one-family dog. His size makes **46** him suitable for city living.

47

Basset

Height: 12½–15 inches (32–38 cm); weight: 40–60 pounds (18–27 kg).

The breed that originated in France, the Basset (from French for low stature) has the head of a Bloodhound, is low to the ground like a big-boned Dachshund, and has the markings of a Foxhound. He is possessed with a remarkable nose, second only to the Bloodhound. When hunting and on the scent, his rich melodious baritone bark always can be distinguished. Although slow moving, he has been used successfully in hunting rabbits. The Basset keeps his nose close to the ground and can be followed easily when working. He is heavier in bone, size considered, than any other breed. Any recognized hound color is accepted, with black, tan, and white the most common. The two-toned Bassets range from pale lemon and white to deep mahogany and white. The coat is hard, smooth, short, and needs no trimming. The Basset is an easy dog to live with, being gentle and placid. Despite his sad facial expression, he is a cheerful, affectionate dog, who gets along well with children. He likes to eat, so watch his waistline.

Beagle

Small: height, 13 inches (33 cm) maximum; weight, 15–18 pounds (7–8 kg).
Large: height, 15 inches (38 cm) maximum; weight, 18–24 pounds (8–11 kg).

Smallest of the hounds, the Beagle is the most popular of his group in the U.S.A. He comes in two sizes. He is a miniature foxhound but solid and big for his size. He is the hunter's number-one dog for rabbits, for his small size gives him tremendous speed. More Beagle trials are held than any other field competition. When he is hunting, especially in a pack, his high tenor bay cannot be mistaken. He is often called the "Singing Beagle." The breed has been known in England since the days of Henry VIII and Queen Elizabeth. The Beagle was imported into the United States in the 1870s. He can be any hound color, the combination of black, tan, and white being the most popular. He has the typical hound head, with drooping ears. The brown or hazel eyes have a gentle, pleading expression. The sloping, muscular shoulders give the appearance of freedom of action. His small size makes him a good choice for the city, although his baying may pose a problem with the neighbors. He adapts quickly to the house, unlike some hounds, but because he likes to roam he may rush for the door. He is especially good with children. Easy to keep clean, the coat needs no trimming.

Black and Tan Coonhound

Height: 22–27 inches (56–68 cm); weight: 50–80 pounds (23–36 kg).

The Black and Tan Coonhound is capable of withstanding the rigors of the seasons and of working in difficult terrain. He immediately impresses an observer with his ability to cover the ground in powerful, rhythmic strides. Generations of breeding have developed this raccoon-and-possum specialist. He keeps his nose to the trail and works entirely by scent, and when he has treed his quarry, he lets the hunter know with a rich roaring bark. As the name implies, the color is coal black with rich tan markings above the eyes, on the chest and legs, and on the sides of the muzzle. The coat is short but dense enough to withstand briars and brambles. The hazel to dark brown eyes, almost round, are not too deeply set, and the low-set ears hang in graceful folds, giving the dog a majestic appearance. This is a hardy, friendly dog, but much better suited for the country than the city. He likes to eat and without work will lose his trim **50** figure.

Bloodhound

Height: 23–27 inches (58–68 cm); weight: 80–110 pounds (36–50 kg).

The Bloodhound is scenting king of the dog world. He has the keenest nose of all breeds. Despite his ominous name, he is a friendly, gentle animal. Had the Bloodhounds caught Eliza fleeing across the ice in *Uncle Tom's Cabin*, they would merely have kissed her, for many are trained to identify the object of their chase by placing their paws on the individual's shoulders and licking his or her face. So positive is the Bloodhound's identification that it is accepted as evidence in a court of law. The most famous tracker was Nick Carter, a Kentucky dog whose identification resulted in more than 600 convictions, one of which was at the end of a trail 105 hours old. However, tracking criminals are the stories that make headlines for the Bloodhound, but actually most tracking is in search of people who are lost. In color, he is black and tan, red and tan, or tawny. He is a powerful dog, who stands over more ground than is usual for hounds. The skin is extremely loose, especially around the head and neck where it hangs in deep folds. The expression is noble and dignified. The Bloodhound is characterized by solemnity, wisdom, and power. He is a country, rather than city, dog. He drools, snores, and frequently has eye problems.

Borzoi

Height: 26–29 inches (66–74 cm); weight: 65–105 pounds (29–48 kg).

The Borzoi (the word means "swift" in Russian) was called a Russian Wolfhound in the United States until 1936. Whereas in America this elegant aristocrat of dogdom frequently is used in high-fashion ads, posing with equally elegant models, in Russia he was bred for courage and was used to hunt wolves. There, before the Revolution, he was also the hound of the nobility. Coursing was the national sport. The Borzoi hunted by sight rather than scent, and needed to possess particular structural qualities to chase, catch, and hold his quarry. He combines sound running gear and strong neck and jaws with courage and agility. The Borzoi is tall and graceful with flowing lines. The long, silky coat is either flat, wavy, or curly. On the head, ears, and on the front of the legs it is short and smooth. Any color or color combination is acceptable. The head is unusually long and narrow with dark, intelligent eyes that are rather soft in expression. The Borzoi is a reserved dog and does not enjoy roughhousing with children. Although he is a clean dog, his shedding presents problems. He will adapt to the city, but he is happier in the country where he can stretch his legs and run.

Foxhound, American and English Harrier

American: height, 21–25 inches (53–63 cm); weight, 50–60 pounds (23–27 kg). English: height, 23–25 inches (58–63 cm); weight, 70–80 pounds (32–36 kg). Harrier: height, 19–21 inches (48–53 cm); weight, 40–50 pounds (18–23 kg).

The American Foxhound traces back to the 17th century, when Robert Brooke brought the first pack to Maryland and became the first Master of Hounds in America. George Washington is said to have owned some. The American Foxhound may be any color. He is primarily a hunting dog that can be used on any ground game, although his specialty is the fox. He has a hard, close, medium-length coat. His sloping shoulders are clean and muscular, and convey the idea of action and strength. He is fast and when running with the pack, he keeps his nose down and will follow a trail for hours.

The English is a larger, slower version of the American. The English, too, has the ability to follow a faint scent and run all day. Foxhunting was the sport of the English aristocracy, and some of the famous packs were those of Lord Sefton and the Duke of Beaufort. There are still more packs in England than in any other country.

In size the Harrier is between a big beagle and a small foxhound. He is an excellent rabbit dog. His head is of medium size, with a bold forehead and plenty of expression. All three breeds most frequently are kept in kennels and run in packs. Whereas they are gentle and friendly, they are much happier in the country where there is plenty of room to run. **53**

▲ English Foxhound ▲ American Foxhound

Dachshund

Standard: height, 9–10 inches (23–25 cm); weight, 18–30 pounds (8–14 kg).
Miniature: height, 5 inches (13 cm); weight, under 10 pounds (4.5 kg).

The Dachshund (''badger dog'' in German) comes in three varieties—smooth, longhaired, and wirehaired — and in standard and miniature sizes. In the United States, both standard and mini compete against each other in the show ring. In England, Canada, and Bermuda the standards and miniatures are separated. The short-legged, long-bodied Dachshund is built low to the ground. He has an intelligent facial expression and a bold, confident carriage of the head. He makes a good, alert watchdog, and he will bark to announce a visitor. He has to be fed with care, lest he gets too heavy. In color, he can be red, black and tan, chocolate and tan, or dappled. In the wire variety, although all colors are permitted, wild boar is the most common. The whole body is covered with a uniformly tight, short, thick rough coat. The eyebrows are bushy and there is a beard. In the smooth, the coat is short, thick, and shining. In the longhaired, the soft, sleek, glistening, often slightly wavy hair gives the dog an elegant appearance. Only the wire needs trimming. The Dachshund is an ideal city dog and a cheerful
54 companion for both young and old.

▲ *Smooth*

▲ Dappled ▼ Longhaired

Greyhound

Height: 28–32 inches (71–81 cm); weight. 60–70 pounds (27–32 kg).

The Greyhound is indeed an ancient breed. Solomon sang its praises in the Bible. So respected were Greyhounds by Egyptian pharaohs and Arabian sheiks, that a birth was an event transcending all else, save that of a son, in his master's household. There is mention of the Greyhound in the works of Ovid and Virgil; Chaucer wrote "Greyhoundes he hadde as swifts as fowels in flight." More recently, the Greyhound is associated with dog racing, a sport that has made great strides in the United States, England, and Australia. Coursing has flourished in England for 200 years and here the Greyhound reigns supreme. The Greyhound may be any color. His coat is short, smooth, and firm in texture. His head is long, narrow, and is fairly wide between the ears. The small ears are thrown back and folded, except when the dog is excited and they become semierect. The dark, bright eyes indicate spirit. The Greyhound feels the cold acutely. He is inclined to be a bit highstrung and reserved with strangers, although he is very loving to his owner.

Irish Wolfhound

Height: 30–34 inches (76–86 cm); weight: 110–170 pounds (50–77 kg).

This is the tallest of all the dogs. He is a rough-coated, grey-houndlike dog, combining power and speed with keen sight. The Irish Wolfhound has a long history: the hounds were brought to Greece by the Celts, in 273 B.C. In 391 A.D. the Roman Consul, Quintus Aurelius Symmachus, thanked his brother for the gift of seven Irish Wolfhounds: "All Rome viewed them with wonder," he wrote. The hound was used to hunt wolves and elk in Ireland. With the disappearance of wild animals and with excessive exporting of the big shaggy dogs, the breed was rapidly becoming extinct in the 19th century. Then Captain George Graham took over and from 1862, the British Army officer worked for two decades to bring back the Wolfhound. The Irish grows faster than a lion cub: at birth he weighs from 1 to 2 pounds (½–1 kg), at three months from 35 to 40 pounds (16–18 kg), at six months 100 to 110 pounds (45–50 kg), and at a year 140 to 150 pounds (64–68 kg). Great size, including height at the shoulder proportionate to body length, is the breeder's goal. The recognized colors are gray, brindle, red, black, pure white, and fawn. The Irish has a commanding appearance, and his movements are easy and active. The dogs are gentle, want to please, and are especially good with children. They need lots of exercise.

Norwegian Elkhound

Height: 19½–20½ inches (49–52 cm); weight: 45–55 pounds (20–23 kg).

An ancient breed, dating from 4,000 to 5,000 B.C., this is the all-purpose dog of Norway. The Norwegian Elkhound accompanied the Vikings on their voyages. He was a courageous hunter and devoted companion. In addition to hunting the elk, for which he gets his name, the gray dog was used on moose, bear, and even as a gun dog and retriever of upland game. In appearance, he is the typical Northern dog. Of medium size and substance, he has a square profile and a broad head with erect ears. The tail is tightly curled and carried over the back. A no-nonsense dog in temperament, the Norwegian is bold and energetic. As a hunter, the dog had the agility and stamina to track for hours in all weather and over rough terrain and then hold big game at bay by barking and dodging attacks. The Norwegian makes an excellent guard dog and always will bark an alarm. Indeed, he is prone to do a lot of barking. A one-man pet, the Elkhound is good in either the country or city but he must be taught from the start what he can and cannot do. He has a double coat: the outer is thick, hard, and weather resistant; the under soft and woolly.

Otterhound

Height: 22–27 inches (56–68 cm); weight: 65–115 pounds (29–52 kg).

The Otterhound is a breed long on pedigree—it dates from the 12th century—but relatively short in numbers. In England, he was greatly favored by the nobility. King Henry II was a Master of Otterhounds, as were a half-dozen other reigning monarchs. The dog was used to hunt in packs, and in the latter part of the 19th century more than 20 packs ran regularly in Britain. The breed was recognized by the A.K.C. in 1910. The Otterhound is a large, rough-coated, squarely symmetrical dog. The length of the hound's body, from the shoulders to the base of the tail, is approximately equal to its height at the shoulders. The bitch may have even a longer body. The standard allows any color but usually the Otterhound is grizzly or sandy, with black and tan in clearly defined spots. The markings resemble a softly shaded Airedale. The double coat is rough on the outer, 3 to 6 inches (7–15 cm) long, and water-resistant on the inner. The dog has webbed feet and is an excellent swimmer. He is endowed with a very good nose, although his trailing is painstaking rather than fast. With a powerful bay, he gives a musical chase. The Otterhound is an affectionate, amiable dog, but can be a fearless fighter if attacked. He is protective of his master and family. Rather a slow learner, he is not easy to train.

Rhodesian Ridgeback

Height: 24–27 inches (61–68 cm); weight: 65–85 pounds (29–39 kg).

This breed gets its name from a ridge on its back, which is formed by the hair growing in the opposite direction from the rest of the coat. The ridge is clearly defined, tapering, and symmetrical. It starts immediately behind the shoulders and continues to a point between the prominence of the hips. The Rhodesian Ridgeback comes from South Africa, where he was developed by the Boers. They wanted a dog to hunt big game (he is sometimes called the African Lion Dog) to guard the farm, to herd the livestock, and to be a companion. The Ridgeback's short, dense coat is sleek and glossy but never woolly or silky. He is wheaten in color, running from light tan to red. The head is flat and rather broad between the ears, and should be free from wrinkles when the dog is in repose. The eyes, moderately well apart, are bright and sparkling, their amber to dark brown color harmonizing with the color of the coat. Strong and muscular, the Ridgeback looks as if he could do a good day's work. He is a clean dog, even tempered and quiet around the house. But he was bred to be aggressive and when walked must be kept on a firm leash, for he is not too friendly with other dogs. This powerful hound is extremely loyal to his master and the family.

Saluki

Height: 20–28 inches (51–71 cm); weight: 40–60 pounds (18–27 kg).

The Saluki has been traced back by archeologists 9,000 years. He is depicted in carvings from the Sumerian Empire and later on Egyptian tombs. A treasured member of mighty households from the Caspian Sea to the Sahara, the Saluki was held in such esteem that he was never sold but exchanged. The first Salukis are believed to have been brought to Europe by the Crusaders. Possessed of tremendous speed and remarkable sight, the Saluki was trained to hunt the gazelle in the most difficult terrain, from deep sand to rocky mountains. The coat is smooth and of soft, silky texture, with feathering on the legs, long ears, and curved low-set tail. He is white, cream, fawn, red, grizzle and tan, black and tan, and tricolor (white, black, and tan). There is also a smooth variety, with no feathering and a finer coat. Clean-cut, graceful, and slender, with a long, narrow head, the Saluki's expression is dignified and gentle, with deep far-seeing eyes. Salukis are inclined to be rather stand-offish with strangers. They are good watchdogs. They like to run and will dart out the door unless watched. **61**

Scottish Deerhound

Height: 28–32 inches (71–81 cm); weight: 75–110 pounds (34–50 kg).

The "Royal Dog of Scotland" has left his pawprint on the pages of history. Such a great value had been placed upon the Deerhound that the breed nearly became extinct. In the Middle Ages, no peer of rank below an earl could own one. At the first Westminster Kennel Club show in New York, in 1877, two Deerhounds "bred by Her Majesty, the Queen of England" were offered for $50,000 each. Sir Walter Scott described his Scottish Deerhound as "the most perfect creature of heaven." The Deerhound resembles a rough-coated Greyhound of larger size and bone. Color is a matter of fancy, but the dark blue-gray is most preferred, followed by the darker and lighter grays or brindles. The oldest strains were yellow and sandy red or red fawn, with black ears and muzzles. Breeders strive for as much height as possible and for an easy-moving dog. The long head is carried high. A thick, close-lying, ragged coat, harsh or crisp to the touch is preferred. Since the Scottish Deerhound was once close to the clan chieftans, he wants human companionship. The big fellow is not very happy in a kennel and makes a much better country than city dog. In the house, he is quiet, affectionate, and keeps out of the way.

Whippet

Height: 18–22 inches (46–56 cm); weight: 26–30 pounds (12–14 kg).

For his size and weight, the Whippet is the fastest dog of all breeds. In racing, he has been timed at up to 40 miles (64 km) an hour. He is a Greyhound in miniature. Although he looks delicate and shivers with the cold, he is fairly robust and rarely needs a trip to the veterinarian. The Whippet is clean and makes a good pet for the apartment dweller. His very short smooth coat doesn't require much attention. Any color is permissible, but white with markings of fawn, blue, black, or brindle are the most common. These shades are also seen in solid colors. The Whippet gives the appearance of elegance, grace, and symmetry of outline. He has a low, free-moving, smooth gait, and covers a maximum distance with a minimum of motion. The long, lean head has small ears that are thrown back and folded, except when the dog is excited and they become semierect. The large eyes have a keen, intelligent, alert expression. The long, tapering tail reaches to the hip-bone, when drawn through the hind legs. Not a particularly demonstrative breed, still he is gentle, obedient, and of good size for riding in a car or taking on a trip.

▼ Police training for German Shepherd ▲ Dog sled races ▼ St. Bernard

▼ Boxer

3
Working

The working breeds consist of three classes: guard, herding, and draft or sled. These are the dogs that stand beside man to lighten his burden, protect his possessions, and herd his livestock. The German Shepherds, Doberman Pinschers, and Rottweilers make excellent guard dogs. Collies, Great Pyrenees, Pulis, Shetland Sheepdogs, and Welsh Corgis long have attended the flocks and herds. Alaskan Malamutes, Samoyeds, and Siberian Huskies are the sled dogs of the frozen North. For the city dweller, the larger breeds are not suitable.

65

Akita

Height: 24–28 inches (61–71 cm); weight: 75–100 pounds (34–35 kg).

The Akita is a descendent of an ancient type of dog from Japan. It takes its name from the Akita Prefecture, the northernmost province of Honshu Island. Once used for hunting, in more recent times the Akita has been engaged as a police dog. Helen Keller is believed to have brought the first Akita into the United States in 1937. The dog may be any color—including white, brindle, or pinto—with or without mask or blaze. He has a double coat, with the outer coat straight, harsh, and standing somewhat off the body; the undercoat soft, dense, and shorter than the outer. The undercoat may be a different color than the outer. The large, full tail is set high and carried over the back or against the flank in a three-quarter full or double curl. The Akita has a massive head in balance with the body, and has small, dark, triangular eyes. The body is longer than high. This is a large, powerful, alert dog, with much substance and heavy bones. Dignified and courageous, he is aggressive toward other dogs and requires a firm hand when being walked. He is excellent as a guard dog. In his native land, the Akita long has been a symbol of happiness and good health. The national dog of Japan is affectionate and loyal to his owner and the family, and thrives on human companionship.

Alaskan Malamute

Height: 23–25 inches (58–63 cm); weight: 75–85 pounds (34–39 kg).

This breed owes its name to the Mahlemuts, those Inuits who lived along Kotzebue Sound in northwestern Alaska. Before the snowmobile and airplane, the Malamute was the freight dog of the Arctic. He could pull tremendous loads over the frozen tundra for longer distances than any of the other Northern breeds. He is a powerful and substantially built dog, with a deep chest and a strong, compact body. He has a thick, coarse guard coat and a dense undercoat, from 1 to 2 inches in depth, oily, and woolly. There is thick fur around the neck. The usual colors range from light gray to black, always with white underbodies, parts of legs, feet, and part of mask markings. The only permissible solid color is white. The broad head has wedge-shaped ears, which erect when alerted. The Malamute moves with a proud carriage. The plumed tail is carried over the back and his head is held high. The eyes have a wolflike appearance but a soft expression. In the summer, he does a great deal of shedding. The Malamute is a friendly dog but he has to be taken in hand early or he will try to get his own way. He requires a lot of exercise.

Bearded Collie

Height: 20–22 inches (51–56 cm); weight: 40 pounds (18 kg).

The shaggy Bearded Collie comes from Scotland, where for years he has worked as a sheepdog and drover, moving cattle. To work in the rainy, cold climate of the Highlands, the Beardie had to be hardy and strong. His long, lean, well-muscled body is the inheritance of days of work. A medium-sized dog, he has a long, abundant, harsh double coat. In color, the Beardie is black, gray (all shades from silver to slate), brown (all shades from sandy to chocolate), and usually has white markings on the feet, legs, chest, head, and tip of tail. The hallmark of the breed is the distinctive beard. His legs and low-set tail are covered with shaggy hair. Overall, the dog has an aura of alertness and action, and on his face is an inquisitive expression. The Beardie is a family dog. He has a deep-seated desire to please, and is quite easy to train. A bit on the sensitive side, he revels in praise and is crushed by rebuke. The Beardie is particularly good with children and will herd them back into their own yard. Although he likes wide open space, he adapts to apartment living.

Belgian Malinois, Belgian Sheepdog, and Belgian Tervuren

Height: 22–26 inches (56–66 cm); weight: 55–75 pounds (25–34 kg).

These are three types of sheepherding dogs registered in Belgium, all similar in height, weight, and conformation. However, the Malinois has a short coat but the other two have long, abundant ones. The Sheepdog is black and the Malinois and Tervuren are rich fawn to mahogany, with black overlay. In the U.S.A., the Belgian Sheepdog is the most popular of the three. The Malinois is one of the rarest of all breeds registered with the A.K.C. The first impression of all three breeds is of well-balanced, square dogs, elegant in appearance, with an exceedingly proud carriage of head and neck. They are strong, agile animals, alert and full of life. In America, most are pets but they retain their inherent quality of protectiveness of their master and his or her property. They are vigilant with strangers and make excellent guard dogs. They all have a characteristic gait, tending to move in a curved rather than a straight line. Both the Sheepdog and the Malinois shed quite a bit. The Sheepdog, which served with the Belgian Army in World War I, has been used extensively by police. Both the Sheepdog and the Tervuren have done well in obedience trials. All three breeds are intelligent and easy to train.

▲ *Belgian Tervuren*
◀ *Belgian Sheepdog*

Bernese Mountain Dog

Height: 21–27½ inches (53–70 cm); weight: 75–105 pounds (34–48 kg).

In his native Switzerland, the Bernese Mountain Dog was once used as a true working dog, drawing small carts with dairy products and weavers' baskets, and also serving as a cattle dog. The Bernese is believed to have been left behind by the Roman armies as they swept through Helvetia in their conquest of Europe 2,000 years ago. The Bernese is a well-balanced dog, active and alert. In body, he is rather short in back, compact, with a broad chest. The soft, silky coat has a natural sheen. It is long and slightly wavy. This striking-looking dog is jet black, with russet brown or deep tan markings on the legs. He has a white blaze up the foreface, a white chest and feet, and brown or tan spots over the eyes. The dark brown eyes are full of fire. The fairly thick tail in repose is carried low, but when alert it is lifted gaily. It must never curl or be carried over the back. Like a Collie, the coat needs regular grooming. The Bernese is very possessive of his master and will guard the property zealously. He is rather distrustful of strangers.

Bouvier des Flanders

Height: 22½–27½ inches (57–70 cm); weight: 80–110 pounds (36–50 kg).

The bearded and mustached Bouvier des Flanders has been known by a variety of names: *Vuilbaard* (Dirty Beard), *Koe Hund* (Cow Dog), *Toucheur de Boèuf* (Cattle Drover), and *Bouvier* (Cowherder). Needless to say, he is used as a cattle dog and a general farmworker. He was used extensively to pull milk carts, and during World War I the Bouvier proved his worth as an Army dog. He is a compact, powerfully built dog of upstanding carriage, with an alert, intelligent expression. His rough, tousled, and unkempt coat is capable of withstanding the most inclement weather. It is a double coat, the outer coat harsh, wiry, and so thick that when separated by hand the skin is hardly visible. The fine, soft undercoat becomes thicker in winter. Despite his heavy coat, brushing once a week is sufficient to handle most of the shedding. In color he ranges from fawn to black. The Bouvier is docile and prefers to stay close to home. His herding instinct is evident when he is with children, for he will round them up.

Boxer

Height: 21–25 inches (53–63 cm); weight: 55–75 pounds (25–34 kg).

The Boxer, which originated near the turn of the century in Germany, is a medium-sized, sturdy dog of square build. He has a short back, strong legs, and a short, shiny, tight-fitting coat. His well-developed musculation is clean and hard. The gait is firm, the stride free and ground-covering, the carriage proud and noble. The head imparts to the Boxer a unique stamp. According to the standard "it must be in perfect proportion to the body, never small in comparison to the overall picture." In color the Boxer is either fawn or brindle. The fawn ranges from light tan to dark red or mahogany, with the deeper shades preferred. The brindle should have clearly defined black stripes on a fawn background. Used by the military and the police, the Boxer is alert, dignified, and self-assured, even at rest. With family and friends, he is playful and affectionate. The Boxer is loyal, protective, and intelligent. He adapts easily to city living and is an excellent watchdog.

Briard

Height: 22–27 inches (56–68 cm); weight: 70–90 pounds (32–41 kg).

The province of Brie in France is famous for its cheese and the Briard. The breed is recorded as early as the 12th century, and even Charlemagne is said to have owned Briards. In France, the Briard long has been used as a sheepdog. His agile movements, described as "quicksilver," enable him to make the abrupt turns, springing starts, and sudden stops required in a good herder. His light gait has been compared to that of a cat, and it gives the impression the dog is gliding along without touching the ground. The Briard has an all-weather double coat. It sheds water, so rain does not bother him, and protects him from extreme cold and heat. All colors are permitted except white, but those most commonly seen are black, various tones of gray, and shades of tawny. The uncut, well-feathered tail forms a crook at the extremity, similar in shape to the letter "J." The outer coat normally does not shed and it is thick enough to catch the short dense inner hairs. So, if the dog is combed weekly, there is little shedding. An excellent memory and an ardent desire to please his owner makes the Briard receptive for training. If this big and powerful dog is going to be with children, the training should start early. He is on the independent side and must be taught who is boss. **73**

Bullmastiff and Mastiff

Bullmastiff: height, 24–27 inches (61–68 cm); weight,
100–130 pounds (45–59 kg). Mastiff: height, 27½–30 inches (70–76 cm);
weight, 170–210 pounds (77–95 kg).

The Bullmastiff, a comparatively new breed, is a cross—60
percent Mastiff and 40 percent Bulldog. Fearless yet docile, he
has great strength and is more active and agile than the Mastiff.
The Bullmastiff is a squarely built, compact dog. He has a large
head, with a fair amount of wrinkles when aroused. His short,
dense coat affords weather protection and is red, fawn, or
brindle in color. He learns faster and is more aggressive than
the Mastiff. The Bullmastiff is inclined to be playful with the
family and must be restrained early lest he becomes too bois-
terous. He is an excellent guard dog.

The origin of the Mastiff is somewhat obscure. Although the
big dog is believed to be a descendant of the Tibetan Mastiff,
he invariably is associated with Britain, where he was used as a
war dog, hunter, and guard. Possessed of a large, symmetrical,
well-knit body, the Mastiff is a combination of grandeur and
good nature, courage and docility. He is characterized by a
massive square head and black muzzle. The outer coat is
moderately coarse, the undercoat is dense, short, and close
lying. In color he can be apricot, silver fawn, or dark fawn
brindle. Big as he is, the Mastiff adapts to a city apartment but
he must be exercised and his diet held down. He also has the
disadvantage of snoring and drooling. He loves the family, is
particularly good with children, and instinctively is protective.

Collie

Height: 22–26 inches (56–66 cm); weight: 50–75 pounds (23–34 kg).

The Collie comes in two varieties — the Rough, by far the more common, and the Smooth. The Rough was a sheepdog in the Scottish Highlands, where the weather was rugged. The Smooth is associated with the cattle-raising industry in Northumberland, England, where he was used as a drover's dog. Both varieties have a strong sense of loyalty and friendliness. The coat is the crowning glory of the rough variety. It is abundant except on the head and legs. The outer coat is straight and harsh to the touch. The undercoat is soft, furry, and so close together that it is difficult to see the skin when the hair is parted. There are four recognized colors: sable and white, with sable (shades from light gold to dark mahogany) predominating; tricolor, predominantly black with white markings and tan shadings; blue merle; and white, which preferably has sable or tricolor markings. The Smooth is similar to the Rough, except for its short, flat coat. As the Collie guarded the flock, so does it guard the family. Extremely faithful, intelligent, and affectionate, he makes a good pet. However, he is subject to Collie eye anomaly. He also sheds the undercoat heavily. He should be combed daily.

75

◀ *Mastiff*

Doberman Pinscher

Height: 24–28 inches (61–71 cm); weight: 60–75 pounds (27–34 kg).

This is a "made-in-Germany" breed, with Louis Dobermann the chief architect. What he produced after 15 years was a compactly built, muscular, powerful breed, with great endurance and speed. The Dobe is elegant in appearance and of proud carriage. He is alert, energetic, determined, and fearless. The long head resembles a blunt wedge in both frontal and profile views. The jaws are full and powerful. The dark brown, almond-shaped eyes have a keen expression. The tail is docked. The smooth, short, hard, thick coat requires little care. The colors are black and tan, red, blue, and Isabella (fawn). This is a breed that has become tremendously popular because of his prowess as a guard dog. He is intelligent and easy to train. Although the Dobe does not look for trouble, he brooks no nonsense. He is suspicious of strangers, and this includes other dogs. Indeed, in the standard it says "an aggressive or belligerent attitude toward other dogs shall not be deemed viciousness." When buying a Doberman it is necessary to choose a breeder with dogs of good temperament.

German Shepherd

Height: 22–26 inches (56–66 cm); weight: 65–85 pounds (29–39 kg).

The German Shepherd is an all-round service dog: he had an enviable record with the K-9 Corps in World War II, he is used extensively by police and customs officers, he does exceptionally well as a guide dog for the sightless, and he is a skilled herder and farmworker. He is a wonderful companion in the home. The Shepherd is the number-one dog in many countries of the world. He is a strong, agile, well-muscled animal, alert and full of life. He is well-balanced, longer than tall, and presents an outline of smooth curves rather than angles. The Shepherd has a distinct personality: he is direct and fearless, but not hostile, self-confident, and somewhat aloof. In appearance, the head is noble, cleanly chiseled, and strong. The Shepherd has a double coat of medium length. In color, he is black and tan, golden sable, gray sable, or all black. The German Shepherd is an extremely intelligent dog and learns quickly. However, he is sensitive, and when being trained, he responds to affection and praise but resents anger. He is subject to hip dysplasia. The German Shepherd is a superb guard dog and will defend his master and property. Because of its popularity, the breed had trouble for a period due to unscrupulous breeders who produced timid, nervous animals. This has largely been overcome but care should be exercised and one should buy from a reputable breeder.

Great Dane

Height: 28–33 inches (71–84 cm); weight: 120–160 pounds (54–73 kg).

Affectionately called the Apollo of Dogs, the Great Dane has been known by many names — the German Mastiff, Deutsche Dogge, Ulm Dog, and Boar Hound. The name Great Dane is somewhat of a misnomer, since the giant breed had its greatest development in Germany, not Denmark. The Dane is an imposing dog, combining majesty, dignity, strength, and elegance with great size and a powerful, well-formed, smoothly muscled body. Spirited and courageous, he is friendly and dependable. The Dane has a short, very thick, smooth, glossy coat. There are five recognized colors: brindle, ranging from light to deep golden yellow with strong black stripes; fawn, golden to deep golden yellow with a black mask; blue, a pure steel blue; black, glossy; and harlequin, pure white with black torn patches irregularly and well distributed over the entire body. The Great Dane adapts to either country or city living, but he should have plenty of exercise. He is a short-lived dog—eight to ten years—and frequently is a victim of bloat. The Dane is subject to hip dysplasia. He is a friendly animal who by his very size would serve as a watchdog. At one time he hunted wild boar but now he is strictly a big pet and does little more than hunt snacks in the kitchen.

Great Pyrenees

Height: 25–32 inches (63–81 cm); weight: 90–125 pounds (41–88 kg).

Designated as the Royal dog of France by Louis XIV, the Great Pyrenees has enjoyed a long, colorful history dating back to the Bronze Age, 1800–1000 B.C. Known in Europe as the Pyrenean Mountain Dog, he served French and Spanish shepherds in guarding flocks. He was also used for centuries as a guard and watchdog on the large estates in France. The first Great Pyrenees were sent to America in 1824 by General Lafayette. The Great Pyrenees is a big, hardy, majestic dog, strikingly beautiful with his all-white or principally white coat, with markings of badger, gray, or shades of tan. His large head is wedge-shaped, measuring 10 to 11 inches (25–28 cm) from the dome to the point of the nose. The coat, created to withstand severe weather, consists of a heavy, fine undercoat and a long, flat outer coat of coarser hair, straight or slightly undulating. He should be groomed at least once a week, and when he sheds there is a lot of hair. He gets along with other dogs, so he is not difficult to walk. He is serious in play and work, adapting to the moods of his master and family. In the home he will settle down quietly in a corner, despite his big size.

Komondor

Height: 23½–25½ inches (60–65 cm); weight: 80–95 pounds (36–43 kg).

For centuries these big dogs guarded sheep and cattle from predatory animals on the *pusztas,* or grassy plains, in Hungary. The Komondor's most unusual feature is his dense corded white coat, which looks like a giant mop. Since he lived in the open most of the year, he needed a coat to protect his whole body. The double coat is weather-resistant and tassellike. The cords on the outer are so thick and dense it would be difficult for another animal to get to the Komondor's throat. Meanwhile, the dog, a fighter, would be chewing the attacker. This is an animal of great strength, with plenty of bone and substance. The tendency for the hair to cord is natural. However, the owner must guide the coat into cords or some will mat. Once corded, grooming is easy, for one never uses a brush. However, the job lies in keeping that white coat clean. After a bath it takes ten hours to dry. He is a guard dog par excellence, and protective of his master, the family, and property. This country dog needs exercise. On the stubborn side, he is a bit difficult to housebreak. This is a dog who never fails to get attention: walk him in the city and you will be stopped every few feet by **80** people inquiring about the breed.

Kuvasz

Height: 26–30 inches (66–76 cm); weight: 70–115 pounds (32–52 kg).

The strikingly beautiful Kuvasz is an ancient breed from Hungary with a history that can be traced back to the Sumerian herdsmen 7,000 years ago. He was used as a sheepdog on the *pusztas*. The big white fellow is a good guard and seems to possess the ability to act on his own initiative at the right time and without an order. He is bold, fearless, has a good nose, and has been used to hunt big game. The Kuvasz is sturdily built, well balanced, neither lanky nor cobby. The double coat is weather resistant and insulates him from both heat and cold. It ranges from quite wavy to straight. A spirited dog of keen intelligence, determination, courage, and curiosity, he is a natural guardian of the family. He is sensitive, and reacts much better to praise than to punishment, for he wants to please. The Kuvasz is especially protective of children. He is polite but rather suspicious of strangers, always keeping an eye on them. An active dog, he needs plenty of exercise.

Newfoundland

Height: 26-28 inches (66-71 cm); weight: 120-170 pounds (54-77 kg).

The Newfoundland is a large, strong active dog, at home on both the land and in water, where he is known for his lifesaving instincts. In sailing days, almost every ship had a Newf aboard. He served as a courier between fishing vessels and in rescue work. During World War II, the big dog was used in the Aleutians to pull sacks of coal and to carry ammunition. On his native island, records show that Newfoundlands hauled wood, loads of fish, and helped with the heavy fishing nets. The outstanding characteristic of the breed is good disposition. For generations, the Newf has been known as the traditional children's protector and playmate. Unlike a smaller dog, he is not easily hurt by small, tugging fingers. The Newf has dignity and a proud head carriage. The dog's expression is soft and reflects the Newf's character—benevolent and intelligent. In color the Newf is black, bronze, or the Landseer type (the black and white dog painted by Sir Edwin Landseer, which bears his name). There is a weather-resistant double coat, the outer being moderately long and full but not shaggy. On the negative side, the Newf is a heavy drooler.

Old English Sheepdog

Height: males minimum 22 inches (56 cm), females less; weight: 75–130 pounds (34–59 kg).

The "old" in Old English is a misnomer, for the breed had its start less than 200 years ago—a newcomer compared to the Saluki or Norwegian Elkhound. At first the Old English was used as a drover's dog, driving cattle and sheep to the market, and to denote their occupation, their tails were bobbed. They became known as bobtails. They have a profuse, shaggy coat, which covers even the eyes, giving the impression of an over-fat dog. The hair is of good hard texture, not straight but free from curls. However, it requires lots of brushing and grooming to prevent mats from forming. The hair over the face interferes with the dog's vision but to compensate he is endowed with acute hearing and a good nose. The Old English is a strong, compact dog of great symmetry, practically the same in measurement from shoulder to stern as in height, and absolutely free from legginess. When he walks or trots, he has a characteristic ambling or pacing movement. In color, he is gray, grizzle, blue, or blue merle, with or without white marking. A good watchdog, he is at home in both the city and country. **83**

Puli

Height: 16–19 inches (41–48 cm); weight: 25–30 pounds (11–14 kg).

When the Magyars came down into the Hungarian plains they brought along a medium-sized, alert dog. He was the Puli, and for many years he has been a true worker—herding the flocks of sheep. He is a dog of great devotion and loyalty to his master's family. He is sensibly suspicious of strangers and therefore an excellent guard. Striking and characteristic is the coat, which for centuries fitted him for the rigors of outdoor life where sheep were pastured. The double weather-resisting coat comes in two varieties—long, straight, and medium textured; wavy or slightly curly and combed out or in tight, tassellike, even cords. The coat mats easily and requires constant brushing. In color, the Puli is solid black, rusty-black, various shades of gray, and solid white. In the U.S.A., he is a pet. In his days with the sheep, he did a lot of barking, and that characteristic remains. Extremely intelligent, the Hungarian learns quickly. He is inclined to be a one-family dog.

Rottweiler

Height: 21½–27 inches (54–68 cm); weight: 85–130 pounds (39–59 kg).

A native of Rottweil in Württemberg, Germany, would not know a Rottweiler of the canine variety by that name but by *Metzgerhund* (Butcher Dog). In the Middle Ages, butchers from Rottweil would tie money belts around the necks of their Rottweilers when they went to purchase cattle. On the return journey the dog would act as a drover for the newly acquired cattle. Now the Rottweiler is used extensively by the police. In Germany, a tight leash is kept on the breeder: before a Rottweiler can be bred, it must have been shown at least three times under two different judges, and have been rated excellent or very good. No more than six puppies are allowed in a litter. This dog, which is black with tan markings, is strongly built and has great power. He is devoted to his master and family and is protective of the children. The Rottweiler must be taken in hand right from the start, for he is a fairly stubborn dog and could be quite a handful if allowed his own way. He is a **84** self-reliant dog, and will not bark needlessly.

St. Bernard

Height: minimum 25½ and 27½ inches (65 and 70 cm); weight: 145–225 pounds (66–102 kg).

This is the breed that won fame as the rescue dog in the snowy Alps, working out of the Hospice of St. Bernard. More than 2,500 saved lives were credited to the noble animals, one of whom, Barry, led to the rescue of 40. In 1830, the St. Bernards at the Hospice, who all were shorthaired, had deteriorated because of too much inbreeding. The monks then brought in some Newfoundlands and from the outcross came the first longhaired variety, which now are so popular. Both types are massive dogs, strong and muscular with a powerful head and a most intelligent expression. The shorthaired has a dense, smooth-lying coat that does not feel rough to the touch. In the long coat, the hair is of medium length, straight to slightly wavy, never curly or shaggy. The tail is bushy, with dense hair of moderate length. There must be a white chest, feet, and top of tail. The well-bred St. Bernard has a sweet disposition and is very good with children. He drools excessively and his coat comes out by the handful when he sheds.

Samoyed

Height: 19–23½ inches (48–60 cm); weight: 45–70 pounds (20–32 kg).

The Samoyed, often called "the white dog with the smiling face," is named after the Samoyed people of northeast Siberia, who bred the dog for centuries. Dr. Fridtjof Nansen, a Nobel Prize winner and Arctic explorer, did much to bring the Samoyed to the attention of the world, using Sams as sled dogs on his expeditions. The white dog presents a picture of beauty, alertness, and strength, along with agility, dignity, and grace. Since he came from a cold climate, his heavy double coat is weather-resistant. The undercoat is soft, short, thick, close wool. Longer and harsher hair grows through it to form the outer coat, which stands straight out from the body. The coat forms a ruff around the neck and shoulders, framing the head. In color, the Sam is pure white, white and biscuit, cream, or all biscuit. The lips are black and slightly curved at the corners of the mouth, giving the "Samoyed smile." The head is wedge shaped, similar to a fox or wolf, and the eyes are almond shaped, probably from squinting in the bright Arctic sunlight for hundreds of years. The Samoyed is a gentle dog and a good companion. He adapts to the city but needs lots of exercise and is on the restless side. He is a heavy shedder.

Schnauzer

Giant: height, 23½–27½ inches (60–70 cm); weight, 70–96 pounds (32–44 kg).
Standard: height, 17–19 inches (43–51 cm); weight, 35–50 pounds (16–23 kg).
Miniature: height, 12–14 inches (30–35 cm); weight, 14–17 pounds (6–8 kg).

The standard and giant varieties of the Schnauzer are both classified as working breeds, the miniature as a terrier. The standard is the oldest of the three members of the family. It gets its name from the bearded muzzle, or *schnauze,* the German word for muzzle or snout. The standard, which goes back to the 15th century, was long used as a guard dog and a ratter. During World War I, he served as a dispatch carrier and for the Red Cross. The giant, bred up from the standard and crossed with sheepdogs, was a drover's dog—Bavarian cattlemen used him to drive their livestock to market. More recently, he has been used by breweries as a guard dog and by the German police. The miniature, bred down from the standard by crossing with the Affenpinscher, is not only the most popular in the family but is number one among all the terrier breeds. A small edition of the standard, he is sturdily built, nearly square in proportion of body length to height with plenty of bone. The typical color for all varieties is salt and pepper in shades of gray. Tan shading is permissible. Black is the only solid color allowed. The standard's rugged build and dense, hard coat is accentuated by the hallmark of the breed: arched eyebrows, bristly mustache, and luxuriant whiskers. The reliable temperament, rugged build, and weather-resistant wiry coat of the giant makes for one of the most useful, powerful, and enduring of the working breeds.

Shetland Sheepdog

Height: 13–16 inches (33–41 cm); weight, 20–30 pounds (9–14 kg).

The Shetland Islands are known for the diminutives — Shetland ponies, cattle, and sheepdogs. In size, the Shetland Sheepdog bears the same relationship to the Collie that the Shetland pony does to the horse. The Sheltie is a small, alert, longhaired dog. He is agile and sturdy. The coat is double, with the outer consisting of long, straight, harsh hair, and the inner being short, furry and so dense that it gives the overall coat a "stand-off" appearance. The hair on the face, tips of ears, and feet is smooth; on the tail it is profuse. There is quite a variety of colors — black; black and white; black, tan, and white; blue merle; and sable (ranging from golden through mahogany) marked with varying amounts of white. The Sheltie, through his years of working sheep, wants to help. He is intensely loyal, affectionate, and responsive to his owner and family. However, he may be reserved toward strangers but will not display fear, just watchfulness. When he sheds, the undercoat comes out in handfuls, so he must be brushed vigorously. He is a good watchdog and will bark an alarm. The Sheltie is a top performer in obedience trials.

89

◄ *Miniature Schnauzer*

Siberian Husky

Height: 20–23½ inches (51–60 cm); weight: 35–60 pounds (16–27 kg).

Most popular of the Arctic sled dogs is the Siberian Husky. Whereas the Malamute is the freight dog of the group, the Husky is the speedster. He gained fame in 1925, when a team of Siberians carried diptheria antitoxin to the stricken city of Nome, Alaska. During World War II, the dogs served with the Army's Search and Rescue unit in the Arctic. The Siberian is a medium-sized working dog, quick and light on his feet and free and graceful in action. His moderately compact and well-furred body, erect ears, and brush tail suggest his Northern heritage. His gait is smooth and seemingly effortless. The expression of his almond-shaped eyes is friendly, interested, and even mischievous. The eyes can be blue, brown, or one of each. The double coat is medium in length, never so long as to obscure the clean-cut outline of the dog. All colors from black to pure white are permissible, but the most usual are silver-gray, tan and black, wolf, and red. The Husky is a wonderful family dog but not a good watchdog, for he loves everyone. He is exceptionally good with children. Bred to work, he likes exercise. He sometimes is hard to housebreak. The Siberian sheds his undercoat heavily. He makes a fine pet.

Welsh Corgi, Pembroke and Cardigan

Pembroke: height, 10–12 inches (25–30 cm); weight, 25–30 pounds (11–14 kg).
Cardigan: height, 10–12 inches (25–30 cm); weight, 28–33 pounds (13–15 kg).

The Corgis, from both Pembrokeshire and Cardiganshire, Wales, were bred to be cattle dogs. They moved the cows by nipping at their heels but had to be agile enough to avoid being kicked. The two varieties are very similar except for the Cardigan's long tail and the Pembroke's tail, which is docked as short as possible. Occasionally the Pembroke is born tailless. The Cardigan is slightly taller and heavier, has a longer body, and has a distinct crook to the forelegs. Both are low-set, strong, and sturdily built. They give an impression of substance and stamina in a small space. They have an intelligent alert, foxy expression, watchful yet friendly. In color, the Pembroke is red (the most popular), sable, fawn, black, and tan. His medium-length coat has a short, thick, weather-resistant undercoat, and a coarser, longer outer coat. The Cardigan's colors are the same except he is also seen with all shades of brindle, tricolor, and blue merle. Both usually have flashings on the chest, neck, feet, face, and with the Cardigan, on the tip of his tail. Both learn quickly and are excellent dogs for an apartment since they are small, obedient, hardy, and loyal. They are great favorites of the British royal family. **91**

▲ *Pembroke*

▲ Bull Terrier ▼ Soft-coated Wheaten ▲ Cairn ▼ Welsh

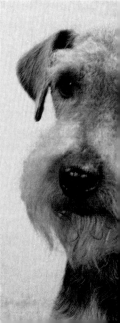

4

Terriers

Most of the terriers carry a "made-in-Britain" label. Their name is derived from the Latin word *terra,* meaning earth, which describes the purpose of these bold, alert dogs. They were bred to be hunters who go underground after their prey. Noisiest of all the breeds, the terrier is an excellent burglar alarm. He has good feet, good teeth, and a punishing jaw. Playful and courageous, terriers have strong wills of their own but when trained make lovable companions. Ranging from the little 10-inch (25-cm) Australian, Cairn, and Norwich to the 23-inch (58-cm) giant Airedale, they all make good house pets and adapt well to city life.

Airedale

Height: 24 inches (61 cm); weight: 55 pounds (25 kg).

Airedale, dubbed king of terriers because he is the biggest, gets his name from England's Aire River in Yorkshire. Most researchers agree that he is a cross between the extinct Old English Black and Tan Terrier and the Otterhound. The Airedale made his debut as a showdog in the late 19th century. He has been used as a hunter, a dispatch carrier in wars, and as a police dog. His head, ears, elbows, and legs up to the thighs are tan. The back is almost completely covered by a black- or dark-grizzled saddle, and he has a long, flat coat. He has V-shaped ears, small dark eyes, and a black nose. The forelegs are perfectly straight, with plenty of muscle and bone. This stylish dog with his elegant, arched neck, has square body proportions. The Airedale is a toughie who brooks no nonsense but still has a sense of humor. His courage is legion, and he has a reputation as protector of his master's family and property.

American Staffordshire

Height: 17–19 inches (43–48 cm); weight: 28–39 pounds (13–18 kg).

It was a cross between a terrier and a Bulldog that produced this breed, and over the years it has been called Half-and-Half, Pit Bullterrier, and Pit Dog. As the names imply, the dog was bred to fight in the pit, and his character encompasses the tenacity and courage of the Bulldog with the agility and spirit of the terrier. Any color, solid or parti, is permissible, with the smooth, glossy coat short, close, stiff to the touch. The ears can be cropped or uncropped, although the latter is preferable. The dark, round, low-set eyes are far apart. The head is medium length, with pronounced cheek muscles. The Staff gives the impression of great strength for his size and is a well-put-together dog, muscular but agile and graceful. His courage is proverbial. He has an excellent temperament, is gentle with children, and is a natural protector of his property. He must be walked on a tight leash lest he lunge at other dogs. **95**

Australian

Height: 10 inches (25 cm); weight: 12–14 pounds (5–6 kg).

One of the smallest of the terrier breeds, almost toy in size, the Aussie is a spirited animal with the aggressiveness of the natural rat killer. However, as a companion he is friendly and affectionate. The outer coat is harsh and straight, about 2½ inches (6 cm) all over the body, with a soft, short undercoat. There is not much shedding. The Aussie has two distinguishing features—a topknot, which covers the top of the skull and which is of finer texture and is lighter in color than the body coat, and a ruff at the neck. The small ears are set high on the skull and well apart. The Aussie may be blue-black or silver black with rich tan markings on the head and legs, sandy colored, or clear red. The most favored color is blue-black with tan markings, although a good red with light topknot is very attractive. The Aussie is not snappy or yappy, say its breeders, and if he is barking, there is a reason. His progenitors are believed to be Cairn, Dandie Dinmont, Scottie, Irish, Skye, and Yorkie. The Aussie is at home in water as well as land.

Bedlington

Height: 15½–16½ inches (39–42 cm); weight: 17–23 pounds (8–10 kg).

The Bedlington takes his name from that mining county in England. He looks like a little lamb, but looks are deceiving —he can be a tiger, should the need arise. Stories are told of how miners in Northumberland wagered large stakes on dog fights in which the Bedlington would battle till death. The miners also wanted a dog who could run down a rabbit and help in badger and foxhunting. Over the years, the dog became a housepet and there are few that would work in the field today. The Bedlington is a lithe, well-balanced dog. The coat is a distinctive mixture of hard and soft hair standing well out from the skin. There is very little shedding. The pear-shaped head is covered with a profuse topknot, lighter than the color of the body. It is set low and never carried over the back, which is roached. The hind legs are longer than the forelegs. Blue and liver are the colors generally seen, although sandy and tan are acceptable. The dog is endowed with great endurance and is capable of galloping at high speed.

96

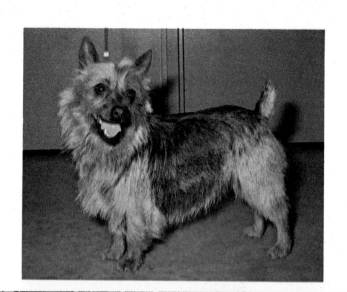

Border

Height: 11½–15½ inches (29–40 cm); weight: 15 pounds (7 kg).

The Border, one of the rarest breeds in the United States, had its origin in the border country between England and Scotland. Here the farmers and shepherds of the Cheviot Hills carefully preserved the strain of terrier so needed to run down the fox, which preyed on their livestock. The little Border, a tireless worker, would also hunt otter and badger. He has a weather-resisting coat to protect him from the rains and mists common to the border country. His hide is loose fitting and very thick. His head is similar to that of his hated foe, the otter. It is moderately broad and flat in skull, with plenty of width between the eyes and between the small, V-shaped ears, which are set somewhat on the side. In color, he can be red, grizzle and tan, blue and tan, or wheaten. Although the Borders have never been very popular, those who own them sing their praises. They claim them to be good-natured, affectionate, obedient, easily trained, and exceptionally good with children. In the field, the Border is as hard as nails and very game.

Bull Terrier

Height: 18 ½ inches (47 cm); weight: 35–55 pounds (16–25 kg).

There are two varieties: white and colored. In the early 19th century, when fights were staged between bulls and dogs, the Bull Terrier was developed. He was a cross between the Bulldog and various types of terriers, and he was found in all colors. In 1862, James Hinks from England introduced a pure white strain, which proved to be an instant success. The dog was taught to defend himself and his master but not to provoke a fight. He became known as "the white cavalier." The colored Bull Terrier was produced by mating a Staffordshire Terrier and a white Bull Terrier. The Bull Terrier can be called the original egghead in the canine world. Looking at the dog full face, the head appears long and strong and is oval, or egg shaped. In profile, it curves gently downward from the top of the skull to the tip of the nose. The coat is short, flat, harsh to the touch, and has a fine gloss. The dog's skin fits very tightly. The small, triangular eyes, as dark as possible, have a piercing glint. They are close set and high on the dog's head. In the colored variety, any coat color other than white is accepted, with brindle the most preferred. The Bull Terrier makes an excellent watchdog. **99**

▲ *Colored Bull Terrier*

Cairn

Height: 9½–10 inches (24–25 cm); weight: 13–14 pounds (6 kg).

A cairn is a heap of stones set up as a landmark, but in the dog world it is one of the boldest and smallest of the terriers. In his native Isle of Skye, he courageously would squeeze through small openings in cairns in pursuit of the otter and fox. The Cairn is one of the most ancient of the Scottish breeds. Although not accepted for registration in Britain until 1910, it is known he existed during the time of Mary Queen of Scots. The A.K.C. gave its approval in 1913. The Cairn's head differs from all other terriers: it is shorter, wider, and well furnished with hair on top, giving a general foxy expression. The small pointed ears, free from long hairs, are carried erectly, set wide apart on the side of the head. The hazel eyes, rather sunken, with shaggy eyebrows have a keen terrier expression. The double coat is weather-resistant so the dog can withstand the wet and cold. He sheds very little and does not need to be trimmed. Even for the show ring he needs only a minimal amount of tidying up. The Cairn may be shown in any color except white. Dark ears, muzzle, and tail tip are desirable. This gay, lively dog makes a fine apartment companion.

Fox Terrier, Smooth and Wire

Height: 15½ inches (40 cm); weight: 16–18 pounds (7–8 kg).

The Fox Terrier has been referred to as the little athlete of the dog world. Both varieties, the Smooth and the Wire, were frequently crossed in the early days. However, they come from separate strains and the crossbreeding long has been discontinued. Because of its skill in driving the fox from a hole, the Fox Terrier was classified as a sporting breed when it was first shown in England. In France, Belgium, and Germany, the dog still is used for hunting. The white color was bred so the terrier could easily be seen and distinguished from a fox or badger. Today the standard still calls for white to predominate. In the Smooth, the coat is flat but hard and dense. In the Wire, the harder and more wiry the texture, the better. On no account should the dog look or feel woolly, and there should be no silky hair. The coat should never give him a shaggy look, which means trips to the professional groomer. Most of the Smooths are either white and black or white and tan. The head is lean and narrow, not wedge-shaped, and the small V-shaped ears drop forward, close to the cheek. The dark eyes are moderately small and full of fire. The Fox Terrier, always on the go, does lots of barking and is a good watchdog. **101**

Wire ▲ Smooth ▲

Dandie Dinmont

Height: 8–11 inches (20–28 cm); weight: 24 pounds (11 kg).

Here is a breed of distinction, for unlike the angular bodies of other terriers, the Dandie has no straight lines and is all curves. Like the Bedlington, the Dandie has a topknot. Since both breeds originated in the border country of England, it is likely that they are related. The Dandie's large domed head is covered with soft, silky hair. There are two distinct colors: pepper (ranging from dark bluish black to a light silvery gray) and mustard (ranging from a reddish brown to a pale fawn). Nearly all Dandies have white on the chest. The hair of the coat, which should be about two inches (5 cm) long, is a mixture of hard and soft, giving a crispy feel to the hand. The coat is a bit of a problem and really takes a professional groomer to do a good job. It was a novel, *Guy Mannering* by Sir Walter Scott, that truly brought the breed to the fore. In the book, published in 1814, there appeared a farmer, Dandie Dinmont, with his mustard- and pepper-colored dogs. They were called Dandie Dinmont's Terriers. The little dog originally was a keen hunter but today his hunting is confined to finding dog biscuits. He is inclined to be stubborn and rather reserved. With his little legs, **102** he is a good size for the city dweller.

Irish Terrier

Height: 18 inches (46 cm); weight: 25–27 pounds (11–12 kg).

One of the three terrier breeds that claim Eire as its home, this hot-tempered terrier has earned the epithet of "daredevil." There is a heedless, reckless pluck about this Irish dog, which is characteristic. He is loyal, loving, and will guard his master or home with utter contempt for danger. He can be quite a handful and must be trained with a firm hand from the start. He may be stubborn and a bit difficult to housebreak. He is bright red, golden red, red wheaten, or wheaten. Puppies sometimes have black hair at birth, but it almost always disappears before the dog is full grown. The dense, wiry coat lies fairly close to the body. The Irish is active and lithe, and moves with great animation. His streamlined build has a graceful, racing outline. The head is long, but in proportion to the rest of the body, with small V-type ears dropping forward. The body is moderately long and should not have a short back. In his native land and in several European countries, the Irish is used to hunt woodchucks or rabbits. He likes the water and can be trained to retrieve. During both World Wars, he was used effectively **104** as a messenger dog.

Kerry Blue

Height: 17½–19½ inches (45–50 cm); weight: 30–40 pounds (14–18 kg).

Although the Kerry Blue had been known in its native County Kerry in Ireland for two centuries, it was not until he was adopted as the Republic's national dog that he came into prominence in the breed ring. Previously, he had been used as a bird dog to hunt small game, to retrieve, and even to herd livestock. The breed was recognized in England in 1922 and two years later in the United States. An excellent guard dog, he will bark an alarm—he has a propensity for barking — and will defend his property. In Britain, the Kerry has been used for police work. Breeders are very concerned about color: any shade of blue-gray, from deep slate to light blue-gray of a fairly uniform color throughout, is correct. The puppies are black when they are whelped but gradually change color as they mature. Up to 18 months of age, deviations from the correct mature color are permissible in the show ring. Solid black is a disqualification. The coat is soft, dense, and wavy. The Kerry has found wide favor among allergy sufferers, for he sheds very little. In Ireland, the Kerry is shown in the natural coat, without any trimming. In the U.S.A., the dog is always groomed. **105**

Lakeland

Height: 13½–15 inches (35–40 cm); weight: 17 pounds (8 kg).

This small, workmanlike dog of square, sturdy build, is friendly, gay, and self-confident. Not until 1921 did he become known as a Lakeland, the breed having originated in the Lake District of England. Previously he had been called a Patterdale, the name of a village, and a Cumberland, after the county in which the breed had its birth. In the Lake District, he was trained to attack the fox, who raided flocks of sheep. The Lakeland was slender enough to squeeze through rocks and to go underground after the offender. The Lakie looks very much like the Welsh, and frequently they are mistaken. He is friendly with the family and children, but he is on the stubborn side and not too easy to housebreak. His coat also requires a bit of work. He has acute hearing and is a good watchdog. In color, the Lakeland is blue and tan, red, or wheaten. He has a rectangular head, V-shaped ears, somewhat oval eyes, and powerful jaws. There is a two-ply, weather-resistant coat, with the outer hard and wiry and the undercoat soft. A good-looking dog with a cock-of-the-walk attitude, the Lakeland stands on his toes as if ready to go. He moves gracefully, with a straight-ahead stride.

Manchester

Standard: height, 17 inches (43 cm); weight, 13–22 pounds (6–10 kg).
Toy: height, 10–12 inches (25–30 cm); weight, 5–12 pounds (2–5 kg).

One of the oldest terrier breeds, the Manchester's forerunners were the old Broken-haired Black and Tan Terriers, which were accomplished rat killers. A breeder mated a terrier and a whippet and the cross proved so successful that others followed. Eventually the Manchester emerged. The breed gained in popularity and soon spread over Britain. At the turn of the century in the United States, the dog was used around stables to keep down the rat population. Although the breed is not very popular in either Britain or America, those who own the Manchester sing their praises. There is a sleek look about the Manchester seen in no other terrier. The smooth coat is close and glossy. The long, narrow head is almost flat and the ears are set close together. The jet black and mahogany tan colors should not blend into each other but should form well-defined lines of color division. A small tan spot is over each eye and on each cheek. The Manchester is a one-family dog, reserved with strangers, and an alert watchdog. He tends to overeat. He comes in two sizes, standard and toy.

Norwich

Height: 10 inches (25 cm); weight: 11–12 pounds (5 kg).

Often called the Cantab Terrier because of his popularity among Cambridge students a century ago, the Norwich is a lot of dog in a little package. Tremendously active and a barker, he is a perfect demon, yet not quarrelsome. He has a lovable disposition and a hardy constitution. The breed was introduced into the United States shortly after World War I. Several dogs were sold to hunt clubs, and the Norwich proved a particularly good rabbit dog. In the beginning these little terriers were red, but now wheaten, black and tan, and grizzle are accepted. Ears can be either prick or drop. Bright, expressive dark eyes are characteristic. The coat is as hard and wiry as possible, lying close to the body, with a definite undercoat. The Norwich requires very little trimming. This alert dog is the right size for an apartment, where he will serve as an excellent watchdog. He is a loyal, one-family dog.

Scottish

Height: 10 inches (25 cm); weight: 18–22 pounds (8–10 kg).

The dour Scottie made his debut on a show bench a century ago. Among the first to exhibit was a breeder from Aberdeen, Scotland, and the breed became known as the Aberdeen, a name that was to stick for a number of years. The Scottish Terrier Club of England was founded in 1883 and that of Scotland five years later. The first Scottie was registered in the United States in 1884. The Scottie can always be heard, for he is a barker. He has a strong will and is inclined to be aloof with strangers. He does not bestow his affection lightly, but once he does he is unswervingly loyal and very protective. It takes a lot of grooming to keep him looking trim. In color, he is black, steel gray, brindle, sandy, or wheaten. But color is not deemed as important as body and coat. The body should be moderately short, well ribbed, with very muscular hindquarters. The coat is rather short, about two inches, and has a dense undercoat with a hard, wiry outercoat. The Scottie has a keen, sharp, active expression. Both the head and tail are carried well up. The dog gives the impression of immense power in a small **108** size. He should show true terrier character.

109

Sealyham

Height: 10½ inches (27 cm); weight: 23–24 pounds (10–11 kg).

"Just as old as the hill is the Sealyham/Mars was his sire and Diana his dam." The little white terrier is not that ancient, however, having been developed by Captain John Edwardes in the mid-19th century. The breed's name is derived from the captain's estate, Sealyham, in Haverfordwest, Wales. The breed is rather a conglomerate, for it is claimed it was evolved from the Welsh Corgi, Flanders Basset, Dandie Dinmont, Bull Terrier, West Highland White, and Wire Fox Terrier. Edwardes wanted a bold dog that would burrow into the earth after his quarry, as well as work above ground. The Sealy was recognized in both America and England in 1911. A white dog, he is permitted to have lemon, tan, or badger markings on the head and ears. The head is long and broad, the jaws powerful and square. The dark eyes, deeply set and fairly wide apart, have a keen expression. The coat is weather-resisting, comprised of a soft, dense undercoat and a hard, wiry topcoat. The Sealy is a smart dog who learns quickly. He requires considerable trimming to keep him looking stylish. Ever keen and alert, of extraordinary substance yet free from clumsiness, he embodies power and determination.

Skye

Height: 11 inches (28 cm); weight: 23–30 pounds (10–13 kg).

Just a short ferryboat ride from the Scottish mainland is the Isle of Skye, famous for the clans Macleod and Macdonald and for a little terrier that bears the name of that 48-mile-long (77 km) strip of land. Although most terriers have attained their present form only in the last century, the long-coated Skye of today almost matches the description written by Dr. John Caius in *English Dogges* four centuries ago. The breed became fashionable in England when it was adopted by the nobility, Queen Victoria owning several. The Skye is twice as long as he is high. He is covered with a profuse double coat that falls straight down either side of the body, parting from head to tail. In moderate climates, there might be difficulty in maintaining this luxurious coat. The undercoat is short, close, soft, and woolly; the outer hard, and 5½ inches (14 cm) long. The color must be of one overall shade at the skin, but may be black, blue, gray, silver, fawn, or cream. The tail is long and feathered. The head is long and powerful, the eyes brown, and the ears may be pricked or drop. Fearless, good-tempered, and loyal, he is friendly with those he knows, reserved and cautious with strangers. His long coat must be brushed regularly.

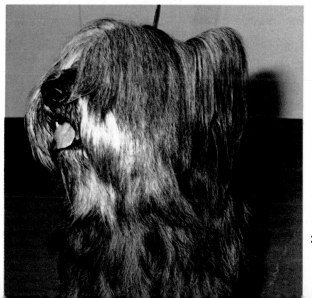

Soft-coated Wheaten

Height: 18–19 inches (46–48 cm); weight: 35–45 pounds (16–18 kg).

Appropriately enough, it was on St. Patrick's Day in 1962 the Soft-coated Wheaten Terrier Club of America was organized and 11 years later received the nod of approval from the A.K.C. In his homeland the breed from Ireland was an all-purpose farmer's dog, who drove and guarded livestock, killed rats, and hunted small game. This medium-sized, well-balanced terrier is abundantly covered with a soft, naturally wavy coat of a good clear wheaten color. The moderately long head is profusely covered with hair. The back is level, with the tail set high and carried gaily. Overall, the dog presents a hardy, active animal, strong and well coordinated. The puppy is born with a dark red or deep brown coat, his face often masked with black. The coat color and texture do not stabilize until 18 to 24 months of age. There has been some controversy about the coat: in the United States the official standard says since the Soft-coated is a natural dog, he should appear so and should not be overly trimmed. In Ireland, he is shown in two coats, trimmed and untrimmed. The Wheaten is a good tempered, game dog, calmer than most terriers, and affectionate.

Staffordshire Bull

Height: 14–16 inches (36–41 cm); weight: 24–38 pounds (11–17 kg).

This English cousin to the American Staffordshire is a somewhat squat, muscular, smooth-coated dog. He should resemble "a square, solid block of concrete." His ancestors are believed to be the Bulldog and the Old English Terrier, now extinct. The Staffordshire Bull came up the hard way. Called the Pit Dog or Pit Bull Terrier, he had an unsavory reputation for fighting and violence. His name became associated with ruffians who cared little for him as a dog but only for his ability in the pit. He comes in a variety of colors: red, fawn, white, black, blue, any of these shades with white, or any shade of brindle with white. The tail is undocked and of medium length. The coat is smooth, short, and close to the skin. The small ears are half-pricked. The Stafford we know today, through careful breeding, quickly becomes a member of the family circle. He is good with children and often is referred to as a "nursemaid dog." In your presence, he will accept visitors but he fears no man or animal and will deter any trespasser. He is powerful, courageous, intelligent, and active. **113**

Welsh

Height: 14–15 inches (36–38 cm); weight: 20 pounds (9 kg).

Although a distinct breed, the Welsh is often called the Airedale's little brother, since he has very similar coloring. In Wales he hunted the badger, fox, and otter. Today, however, he is almost always only a housepet, but with very little training he could be used as a gun dog. He also excels in the water. This alert little dog requires regular grooming. The Welsh is a dog for either the city or country. His black and tan or black grizzle and tan color is very much a plus because he does not have to be bathed as much as the white-coated terrier. Although he does not look for trouble, he is quite capable of holding his own should the need arise. In the early years, the black and tan was quite leggy but he has been bred down into a short-bodied, compact dog. The head is wider between the ears than the Wire Fox Terrier. The expressive dark eyes indicate plenty of pluck. The small V-shaped ears are set fairly high. The hard, wiry coat is very close and abundant. Gay and volatile, the Welsh is affectionate and learns quickly. However, he is pretty much of a one-family dog.

West Highland White

Height: 10–11 inches (25–28 cm); weight: 15–18 pounds (7–8 kg).

As Scottish as a bagpipe but not nearly as dour as some of the other terriers from that land is the West Highland White. Like so many breeds, the little white-coat earlier had been known by different names: the Roseneath, from the estate of the Duke of Argyll; and the Poltalloch, from that community in Scotland where the Malcolm family bred the strain. The white color was purposely bred so the little terrier could easily be distinguished during the hunt. The Highlander is a fiesty little terrier, extremely outgoing and anxious to please. He has a double coat, the outer consisting of straight, hard hair, about two inches (5 cm) long, with less on the neck and shoulders. The head is fairly broad but in proportion to the powerful jaw. The small ears are carried tightly erect. The dark eyes, widely set apart, are sharp and intelligent. The body is compact, and of good substance. The relatively short tail, when standing erect, never should extend above the top of the head. Movement is free, straight, and easy all around. This self-reliant and friendly Highlander is easier to groom than most terriers. He is inclined to be a picky eater.

▲ Pug ▼ Pomeranian ▲ Papillon ▼ Yorkshire Terrier

5

Toys

These are the little dogs usually produced by selective breeding for size. They weigh from 1½ to 18 pounds (.7–8 kg). Spunky, alert, gentle-mannered, and affectionate, they have been household pets for hundreds of years. Although some are fragile looking, they are fairly hardy and generally are long-lived. Most pampered of all the breeds, they are frequently difficult to housebreak. Several of the toys have a pushed-in nose and consequently are likely to wheeze and snore a good deal. They never have done any work and have been bred solely as pets to make their owners happy. They are good dogs for the apartment-house dweller. **117**

Affenpinscher

Height: 10½ inches (27 cm) maximum; weight: 7 –8 pounds (3 kg).

In this dog's native land of Germany, *Affen* means monkey. He gets the monkey label from his chin tuft and mustache, and his expression. Indeed in France he sometimes is called the *Diablotin Moustachu,* or mustached little devil. Some experts believe he has been bred from other small German wirehaired dogs. He has much of the terrier spirit. The Affenpinscher has a round head, not too heavy, with a well-domed forehead, which is covered with long coarse, tangled hair. The coat is very important. It is hard and wiry, looser and shaggier on the eyes, nose, and chin, giving a typical monkey appearance. The best color is black, matching his eyes, but black with tan, red, and gray markings or other mixtures are allowed. The straight back is about equal in length to the height at the shoulder. The Affen is a small dog, the smaller the better. Lively around the house and intelligent, he is easy to teach although somewhat hard to housebreak. Gentle and affectionate, he is a good little watchdog and will bark if anyone approaches the house. Despite his coat, he feels the cold. Some grooming and plucking is required.

Brussels Griffon

Height: 12 inches (30 cm) maximum; weight: 8–10 pounds (3–4 kg).

This bewhiskered little fellow is of Belgian origin and achieved popularity partly because he was a favorite of Queen Maria Henrietta and later Queen Astrid. He is an intelligent, alert, sturdy dog, with a short, thick-set body. The Griff comes in two varieties: the rough, which is by far the most popular, and the smooth. The rough coat is wiry and dense, the harder the better. Never should it feel or look silky or woolly. The rough coat can be reddish brown, with a little black at the whiskers and chin permissible; black and reddish brown mixed, usually black mask and whiskers; black with uniform reddish brown markings; or solid black. The colors of the smooth are similar, except all black is not allowed. The Griff is a friendly dog, extremely intelligent, and a good traveler. The smooth coat is similar to that of the Boston Terrier or Bulldog, with no trace of wire hair. It requires almost no grooming but the roughs must be brushed or trimmed. The Griff is inclined to bark, and if he sleeps on your bed, you will hear him snore. He is not fond of a leash and should be trained to one early.

Chihuahua

Height: 4–5 inches (10–13 cm); weight: 6 pounds (3 kg) maximum.

The smallest of all the breeds is the Chihuahua. He barks more than most dogs, and with good reason—so he will be noticed. He is a good size for a small apartment and excellent as a pet for an older person, since he requires little exercise. By the same token, this is not a breed for children. He feels the cold acutely and likes no better place to sleep than on his master's bed. That can be a trial, too, for the little dog snores and wheezes. The Chihuahua comes in long- and smooth-coated varieties. In the smooth, the close, glossy coat is soft textured. In the long, the hair also is of soft texture, either flat or slightly curly. The ears are heavily fringed, and there is feathering on the feet, legs, and tail. There is a large ruff on the neck. Any color—solid or marked is permissible. The breed's origin is obscure. Most authorities maintain it came from Mexico, but others hold that it originated in Egypt and was then taken to the Mediterranean countries, flourishing on Malta. The Chihuahua belies his delicate appearance for he seldom is ill and lives longer than most dogs. However, he has a predisposition to bad teeth.

English Toy Spaniel

Height: 9–10 inches (23–25 cm); weight: 9–12 pounds (4–5 kg).

There are two varieties of the English Toy Spaniel: the King Charles and Ruby types, which comprise one show variety are solid-colored, and the Prince Charles and Blenheim, which are shown together, are broken-colored dogs. The King Charles is a black and tan (considered a solid color), the black rich and glossy with deep mahogany tan markings over the eyes and on the muzzle, chest, and legs. The Ruby is a solid rich chestnut. The Prince Charles is a tricolor of white, black, and tan. The Blenheim is white with bright red chestnut markings evenly distributed in large patches. The ears and cheeks are red, with a blaze of white extending from the nose up the forehead. In the center of the blaze is a clear red spot the size of a dime, a feature of the Blenheim. The coat for all the English Toy Spaniels is long, silky, soft, and wavy. There is a profuse mane, extending well down the front of the chest. There is heavy feathering on the long ears and on the feet. In compactness of shape these toys almost rival the Pug, but the length of the coat adds to the apparent bulk. He is sturdily built, a good companion, and is well suited as an apartment dog. His long silky coat requires grooming to avoid matting.

Italian Greyhound

Height: 13–15 inches (33–38 cm); weight: 6–10 pounds (3–4 kg).

The Italian Greyhound is small in stature but long in historical background. He has existed in his present form for more than 2,000 years and was a favorite in the days of Pompeii. He was so loved that two statues honor him in the Vatican. Among his owners were Cleopatra, Charles I of England, and Frederick the Great of Prussia, who said, "The more I get to know people, the more I like my dogs." The elegant, graceful I.G. is a miniature edition of the English Greyhound. The arched neck, combined with sloping shoulders and long slender legs, give the dog an appearance of fragility. Perhaps that was the reason a Roman warned *Cave Canem* (beware of the dog). Possibly he was concerned not that his huge chained Mastiff might attack a stranger but that a visitor might step on his tiny pet. The I.G. has a short, glossy, soft-to-the-touch coat that only requires brushing every couple of days. Any color and markings are acceptable, except tan and brindle markings. The running the dainty dog does around the house is almost enough exercise. The Italian Greyhound is sensitive to the cold. Strictly a pet and somewhat high-strung, he is not a dog for a youngster.

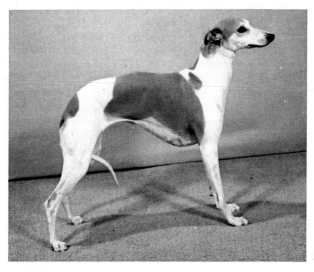

Japanese Spaniel or Japanese Chin

Height: 9 inches (23 cm); weight: 7 pounds (3 kg).

This is a smart, lively dog, with dainty appearance, compact, stylish carriage, and a profuse coat. Long a favorite of the Japanese imperial family and the court, now he has been passed down to the citizens of that land, where he is one of the most popular breeds. The Japanese Spaniel comes in two combinations: white and black, or white and red. However, red includes all shades of sable, brindle, lemon, and orange. The brighter and clearer the red the better, with the white predominating. The long, silky coat is free from wave or curl and has a tendency to stand out, especially on the neck. This gives a thick mane or ruff, which with profuse feathering on the thighs, legs, and tail, give the Japanese a showy appearance. The head is large for the size of the dog, and the length of his body is about its height. The bones of the legs are small, giving them a slender appearance. The little dog carries his richly fringed tail proudly curved over his back. The Japanese Spaniel is intelligent, alert, and friendly. The coat is easy to maintain and just a few minutes of brushing daily will keep him glossy and free of mats. He needs little exercise. Like so **124** many short-nosed breeds, he may snore.

Maltese

Height: 5 inches (13 cm); weight: 7 pounds (3 kg) maximum.

Despite its name, there is much controversy over the history of
the breed. The name refers to Malta but it is claimed by some
authorities that the Maltese, whose history is traced back more
than 3,000 years, may have been shipped through the ports of
the island rather than having originated there. The breed has
been depicted over the centuries in and on tombs and
ceramics of the Egyptians, Greeks, and Romans. An 18th-
century sculpture of the little dog is in the courtyard of the
Tower of London. This tiny toy is covered from head to foot
with a mantle of long, silky white hair. The single coat is parted
down the back, falling down the sides to the ground. The eyes
are very dark, the black rims enhancing the gentle yet alert
expression. The nose also is black. The tail is a longhaired
plume carried gracefully over the back. When the Maltese
moves with his jaunty gait, the coat swoops back like a flowing
gown. An active little dog, he is lively and playful. The Maltese
is affectionate and among the gentlest mannered of all toy
dogs. But the coat gives problems for it must be brushed and
combed daily and the little dog must be bathed regularly to
keep the hair white. **125**

Miniature Pinscher

Height: 8–11 inches (20–28 cm); weight: 6–8 pounds (3–4 kg).

This little German dog is often called a miniature Doberman. In his native land he was named *Reh Pinscher,* because of his resemblance to a very small species of deer. The Min-Pin is structurally a well-balanced, sturdy, compact, dog. The characteristic that identifies him from other toy dogs is his hackney gait. Indeed, he is often called the "poor man's hackney pony." He has a smooth, hard, short, shiny coat. The tail is set high, held erect and docked from ½ to 1 inch. In color, the Min-Pin is solid or stag red, shiny black with sharply defined tan, rusty red markings on the cheeks, lips, lower jaw, lower half of forelegs, and inside of hind legs. The Min-Pin is intelligent, easy to housebreak, and a good watchdog. He is animated, self-possessed, and playful with the owner's family though suspicious of strangers. The slick coat is easy to groom but it does not provide much protection against the elements, for the dog feels the cold. He is an enthusiastic eater.

Papillon

Height: 8-11 inches (20-28 cm); weight: 6-8 pounds (3-4 kg).

Here is a butterfly that barks, has a cold nose, and wags its tail with great animation. *Papillon* is French for butterfly. The breed gets its name from its ears, which are fringed and carried high and well apart so that they resemble the open wings of a butterfly. Although the breed as a whole carries the Papillon appendage, there is also a drop-eared variety, known in Europe the Epagneul Nain. The Papillon was the fashionable pet of the 18th-century French court. The tiny toy is a friendly, elegant dog of fine bone structure; light, dainty, and of lively action. The coat always is parti-color—white with patches of any color. On the head, any color other than white must cover the back and front of both ears and extend without interruption over the eyes. The abundant coat is long, fine, and silky. There is no undercoat. The hair needs brushing and combing to keep it glossy. The Papillon is a hardy, long-lived dog and is much better for adults than children. Extremely intelligent, he is easy to train and has done very well in **126** obedience trials.

Pekingese

Height: 7–8 inches (18–20 cm); weight: 14 pounds (6 kg) maximum.

The Pekingese has been traced to the Tang Dynasty in China. The official standard for the breed says he must suggest his Chinese origin by the individuality of his expression. He should resemble the lion in independence and imply courage, boldness, self-esteem and combativeness, rather than prettiness, daintiness, or delicacy. That is a big order but the Lion Dog, as he is called because of his massive chest and heavy mane, fills the bill for he certainly is no lap dog. Inclined to be rather aloof with strangers, he is devoted and affectionate with his owner and the family, although never yielding his personality. The Peke has a magnificent long and straight coat, with a thick undercoat. The mane extends beyond the shoulder blades, forming a ruff around the neck. All colors are allowed. The coat, of course, must be brushed and combed often to prevent matting. The Peke is inclined to be a choosy eater, and if he sleeps in the same room with you, his snoring may keep you awake. He has a short, flat nose, and large, protruding eyes. The Peke is good for apartment living. He does not chew **128** furniture, and with his loud bark he is a fine watchdog.

Pomeranian

Height: 5–6 inches (13–15 cm); weight: 3–7 pounds (1.4–3 kg).

This dog gets its name from Pomerania, the land on the Baltic Sea. However, most authorities agree that this breed of great antiquity descended from the Spitz and was bred down from the great sled dogs of the Arctic family. The early imports from Pomerania to England were 30-pounders (14 kg) but the size gradually was reduced. When Queen Victoria acquired some of the Poms, the breed received a boost. The coat is the hallmark of the breed. It is double, with a short, thick underpart and a longer, coarse, glistening outercoat, consisting of guard hairs that are harsh to the touch. The coat forms a frill of straight, profuse hair. The front legs are well feathered, and the tail is rich and carried over the back. Any color is acceptable. The Pom is a dainty little dog and a great favorite for the city dweller. He is a pet for adults, not for children, and must be taught from the start who is the master. Daily grooming is necessary to keep the coat in shape. Extremely vivacious, the Pom is inclined to bark quite a bit. He also sheds a good deal. His breeders say he is a lot of dog in a small package.

Pug

Height: 13 inches (33 cm); weight: 14–18 pounds (6–8 kg).

There is a good deal of uncertainty in the origins of many breeds, and so also is there in the early history of the Pug. Some claim it originated in China, others say Russia. However, it did arrive in England from Holland when William and Mary ascended the throne in 1689. It was often called the Dutch Pug. More recently, he was a great favorite with the Duke and Duchess of Windsor. Today he has become a popular pet. Sturdier than most of the toy breeds, the Pug is always ready for a romp and he is extremely anxious to please. Not a delicate dog, he is well put together, and if kept in shape, there is compactness of form and hardness of muscles. The Pug's massive head almost looks too big for the short body. On the face, wrinkles give it a quizzical expression and there is a black mask, the more intense and well defined the better. The smooth, fine coat is short and glossy, and the color is silver, apricot-fawn, or black. The Pug has a very loose skin. With his short nose and pushed-in nostrils, he has breathing problems and wheezes and snores. Not streamlined for running, he requires very little exercise. He also suffers from excessive heat and has a predisposition to ear infections. Since the Pug likes to eat, many tend to get overweight.

Shih Tzu

Height: 8–11 inches (20–28 cm); weight 9–16 pounds (4–7 kg).

The Shih Tzu (Chinese for lion) was a pet of the Imperial Court of another age but it is believed to have originated in Tibet. The little dog is active, alert, and has a distinctly arrogant carriage. He walks with his head high and his heavily plumed tail carried over his back. Although recognized in the United States only in 1969, the Shih Tzu (pronounced *sheed-zoo*) has become popular, which is not always an advantage, for the resulting overbreeding sometimes tends to diminish quality. The dog, while independent in spirit and regal in bearing, is good-natured and affectionate. In appearance, he has a broad, round head with hair falling over the eyes. The large, round dark eyes do not protrude and have a warm expression. All colors are permissible, although in China the most popular was gold, the color of the court. The coat is long, luxurious, and dense, with the hair around the face usually brushed up on the forehead to form a topknot. The coat requires extensive grooming and must be lightly brushed daily, with a thorough grooming once a week to keep it from matting. He is good for a city apartment, being small and an alert watchdog. The Shih Tzu is friendly and craves human companionship more than most breeds. He is not a dog to be left alone all day.

Silky Terrier

Height: 9–10 inches (23–25 cm); weight: 8–10 pounds (4 kg).

This is a cross between the Australian Terrier and the Yorkshire Terrier. The dog was known as the Sydney Terrier, after the town where the breed originated, and was first shown in 1907. The name then was changed to the more inclusive Australian Silky Terrier. In the United States, it is a Silky Terrier. From the Yorkie he inherited the beautiful silky coat, although not nearly as long, and from the Aussie, he has ruggedness and spirit. The Silky is a lightly built, moderately low-set dog, with a strong, wedge-shaped head. The small dark eyes are piercingly keen in expression. The docked tail is well-coated but without plume and is carried erect or semierect. The coat is flat, and as indicated in the breed's name, silky in texture, with the desired length from five to six inches (13–16 cm). On the top of the head, the hair is so profuse as to form a topknot. The hair is parted on the head and down over the back to the root of the tail. In color, the Silky is blue and tan. Without an undercoat there is not much shedding, and a brushing every couple of days will keep him in shape. He is an active little fellow, an excellent watchdog, and quite noisy.

Yorkshire Terrier

Height: 6½–7½ inches (17–19 cm); weight: 7 pounds (3 kg) maximum.

The Yorkshire Terrier was originally called a Scotch Terrier and was not accepted under its current name by The Kennel Club in England until 1886. In the United States the breed has forged steadily ahead so that it is one of the most popular city breeds. The Yorkie is a longhaired toy, whose blue and tan coat is parted on the face and from the base of the head to the end of the tail. It flows evenly and straight down each side of the body. He carries his head high and has an air of self-confidence. Color is important, a rich golden tan on the head and ears, a dark steel blue—not a silver blue—extending over the body from the back of the neck to the root of the tail. The hair on the docked tail is a darker blue. The chest and legs are a bright rich tan. The hair is glossy, fine, and silky. The Yorkie is not a dog for children. The coat of this pet requires a daily brushing for at least five minutes, and much more for a show-dog. The Yorkie is small enough so that he is easy to take on trips. The little dog has acute hearing and will bark a welcome or an alarm. He needs very little exercise, the running he does in the apartment or house being quite sufficient. **133**

▼ White Poodle ▲ Dalmation and pup ▼ Lhasa Apso

6
Nonsporting

The name for the group is somewhat of a misnomer, since the Poodle, long the most popular breed in the United States, originally was a sporting dog, bred to retrieve. Several breeds that once were in this division later were moved to other groups. Although the nonsporting animals are considered as companion dogs, at one time they were bred for a particular purpose. Thus the Bulldog baited the bull, the Dalmatian accompanied the carriage, and the Schipperke and Keeshond were guardians of the barges on the canals in Belgium and Holland. If the powers that control the sport of dogs are at a loss how to classify a breed, it is put into this group—a bit of a hodgepodge. **135**

Bichon Frise

Height: 8–12 inches (20–30 cm); weight: 10–15 pounds (4.5–7 kg).

This sturdy little dog traces his origin to the Canary Island of Teneriffe and for a time was called a Bichon Teneriffe. He was a favorite of the French court in the 16th century. The present name was bestowed upon the breed by Mme. Denise Nizet de Leemans, a noted breeder and judge from Belgium. The Bichon Frise (pronounced *Bee-shohn free-zey*) is solid white, or white with cream, apricot, or gray on the ears or body. He has dropped ears covered with long flowing hair. The large dark brown or black eyes, with black rims, are round, expressive, and alert. Both the lips and nose also are black. The profuse coat is silky and loosely curled, and there is an undercoat. His tail, covered with long flowing hair and carried gaily, is curved to lie on the back. In grooming, the little dog is scissored to show the eyes and to give a full-rounded appearance to the head and body. Properly brushed, there is an overall "powder-puff" look. The Bichon has a stylish gait and a cuddly charm. He likes everyone and is good with children, except he is a little small for any rough play. The coat requires daily brushing and combing and there have to be trips to the professional groomer for the necessary trimming.

Boston Terrier

Height: 14–15 inches (36–38 cm); weight: 25 pounds (11 kg) maximum.

The Boston Terrier, a cross between the Bull Terrier and the Bulldog, was originally called an American Bull Terrier. However, when a group tried to register the breed with the A.K.C., dogdom's ruling body objected to the name, claiming that there already was a Bull Terrier. Since the breed centered around Boston, the name was changed to Boston Terrier and was accepted by the A.K.C. in 1893. The breed has enjoyed success and was America's most popular dog from 1929 through 1935. The Boston is a lively, highly intelligent, compactly built, short-tailed dog. He has a short, smooth, bright coat that is pleasant to touch. It can be brindle with white markings, which is preferred, or black and white. Markings are important with the breed, and ideal is a white muzzle, even white blaze over the head, collar, breast, and part or whole of the legs. He is a good dog for either the city or country, requiring very little grooming and being friendly and affectionate. He has a great deal of terrier in him and likes to play, particularly with a ball. Because of the short nose, he has breathing problems and wheezes and snores. **137**

Bulldog

Height: 14–16 inches (36–41 cm); weight: 40–60 pounds (18–27 kg).

The Bulldog, which gets its name from the "sport" of bull-baiting, for which it was bred, is beautiful for its ugliness. He inspired Cole Porter to write "Bulldog," the song that has echoed across the Yale Bowl gridiron for so many years. Affectionately called a sourmug, he has a smooth coat, a heavy, thick-set body, a massive short-faced head, wide shoulders, and sturdy short legs. The short tail may be either straight or twisted. The skin is soft and loose, especially on the head, neck, and shoulders. The head and face are heavily wrinkled. The general appearance suggests great stability, vigor, and strength. The color of the coat should be uniform, pure of its kind, and brilliant. The most preferred colors are, first, red brindle, then all other brindles, solid white, solid red, solid fawn, and piebald. The Bulldog's gait is a loose-jointed, shuffling, sideways motion, giving a characteristic roll. The gentle old sourmug loves everyone and he is good with the small fry. He is obstinate and will do things at his own speed, which is not very fast, but he wants to please and once he learns something he never forgets it. Because of his pushed-in nose, he has difficulty in hot weather, and he drools and snores.

Chow Chow

Height: 19–20 inches (48–51 cm); weight: 55–70 pounds (25–32 kg).

This ancient breed from China is the only one to have a blue-black tongue. The name is believed to be derived from pidgin English. When masters of sailing vessels in the 18th century had to describe various curios they were bringing back from the Orient, they would simply write "chow chow," rather than list all the items. The canine Chow Chow is a powerful dog, active and alert, with strong muscular development. Looking like a lion, he is a masterpiece of beauty, dignity, and untouched naturalness. His massive head and magnificent coat are his most striking characteristics. He looks out in a lordly manner, scowling, discerning, sober, and snobbish. The coat is dense, abundant, straight, and off-standish. It is rather coarse in texture, with a soft, woolly undercoat. He should be brushed daily. Any color is allowed, with red the most popular. The independent Chow Chow has a strong will of his own. He must be taken in hand early but he responds to a quiet voice and gentle handling much more than to harshness. He is quiet in the house. Wary of strangers, the Chow is devoted to his owner and is an excellent watchdog.

139

Dalmatian

Height: 19–23 inches (48–58 cm); weight: 45–65 pounds (20–29 kg).

The Dalmatian is known by a number of names — the Fire House Dog, Plum Pudding Dog, Coach Dog, Carriage Dog. He long has been associated with the horse, and in the late 18th century in England and France he always was seen trotting alongside the carriages. The Dal also has been used as a bird dog and retriever and as a circus performer. The breed gets its name from Dalmatia, now part of Yugoslavia. The Dal is a strong, muscular, active dog. Extremely intelligent, he learns quickly and does very well at obedience trials. Symmetrical in outline, poised and alert, he is capable of great endurance, combined with a fair amount of speed. The dog has a short, hard, dense coat, sleek and glossy in appearance. His markings are his most distinctive point. He is white with either black or liver spots. The spots should not intermingle but be round and as well defined as possible. The puppy is born pure white, the spots developing early. The Dalmatian requires little grooming and he washes himself like a cat. A good family dog who wants to please, he revels in play with children. He is quiet and if he barks there is a reason. A good traveler, he is **140** always ready to go.

French Bulldog

Height: 11–12 inches (28–30 cm); weight: 28 pounds (13 kg) maximum.

The French Bulldog is the result of a three-nation play. Lace workers from England, where the breed originated, moved to France, bringing their little bulldogs with them. These were crossed with local breeds, and the French Bulldog emerged. He attained his distinctive bat ears on the insistence of American breeders. At first there were two types of ear—the bat, which is erect, broad at the base; elongated, with a round top; and the rose, a small drop ear. In the United States, the Frenchie breeders wanted the bat ear as a stamp of the breed, maintaining the rose made the dog look like a miniature Bulldog. The American influence prevailed, and the bat ears with the large, square, flat head are today characteristic of the Frenchie. His skin is soft and loose, especially at the head and shoulders, forming wrinkles. The coat is brilliant, short, and smooth. Brindle, fawn, white, and brindle and white are acceptable colors. A clean dog, he needs very little grooming and a quick brushing daily is adequate. They are particularly good for senior citizens for they bark very little, though they are fine watchdogs, and don't require too much exercise. The pushed-in nose causes them to snore.

Keeshond

Height: 17–18 inches (43–46 cm); weight: 35–40 pounds (16–18 kg).

Barge dog of the Netherlands and a favorite of the Dutch farmers, the Keeshond is a descendent of an Arctic breed. The Keeshond (pronounced *Cays-hond*) is a handsome dog, who attracts attention not only with his alert carriage and intelligent expression on his foxlike face, but also for his luxurious coat and his richly plumed, tightly curled tail. His double coat is thick around the neck, forepart of the shoulders, and chest, forming a lionlike mane. His rump and hind legs are also thickly coated, forming the characteristic "trousers." The hallmark of the breed are the "spectacles"—a delicately penciled line slanting slightly upward from the outer corner of each eye to the lower corner of the ear, coupled with distinct shadings to form short but expressive eyebrows. In color, the Kees is a mixture of gray and black. The undercoat is a pale gray or cream. The hair of the outer is black-tipped, the length of the black tips producing the typical shading of color. The Kees is a one-family dog, and from his years of serving as a watchdog on the barges he is very protective. He has exceptionally good hearing. The coat requires twice-a-week treatment with a stiff brush.

Lhasa Apso

Height: 9–11 inches (23–28 cm); weight: 15–17 pounds (7–8 kg).

From the sacred Tibetan city of Lhasa comes the Lhasa Apso, called in his native land *Apso Seng Kye,* the Bark Lion Sentry Dog. He is said to have been given the name because, alerted by his acute sense of hearing, he would bark an alarm. The Lhasa has a heavy, straight, dense coat of good length, sometimes trailing on the ground. This was developed over the centuries for a practical reason. For the long winters he had a soft, rich undercoat, topped by a hard outer. Thick hair grew between the pads of the feet, serving as cushions for the rough, frozen terrain. Since there frequently were high winds and much dust, the fall of the hair protected the eyes. In color, the golden or lionlike is preferred, followed by honey, dark grizzle, slate, smoke, parti-color, black, white, and brown. The Lhasa is often three or four years old before the full coat comes. Although small, he is a sturdy, assertive little fellow, who likes to play with the family. On the other hand, he will lie on the floor for hours, near his owner, and be absolutely quiet. The Lhasa is wary of strangers, perhaps a carry over from his years as a sentry. He should be brushed daily to prevent tangles and mats from forming. **143**

Poodle

Standard: height, over 15 inches (38 cm), preferred 22–26 inches (56–66 cm); weight, 45–60 pounds (20–27 kg). Miniature: height, 11–15 inches (28–38 cm); weight, 14–18 pounds (6–8 kg). Toy: height, 10 inches (25 cm) maximum; weight, 5–7 pounds (2–3 kg).

America's most popular dog for years, the Poodle comes in three sizes and a wide variety of colors. He also keeps the grooming salons in business for although the owner can learn how to trim his pet, most patronize a professional to keep their poodle looking chic. This unusually intelligent breed takes many honors in obedience trials. He learns quickly and he has a sense of humor, sometimes deliberately misbehaving if he thinks it will get a laugh. Poodles are friendly, gentle, and very good with youngsters—except that the toy is too fragile for the small child. The standard was bred to be a retriever and he is a good water dog. Indeed, in France he is called *Caniche*, derived from *canard* (duck). He is rather reserved with strangers and a very good watchdog. He is elegant looking, squarely built, well proportioned, and he carries himself proudly. The profuse coat is of harsh texture, and dense through. There are several acceptable clips, depending upon the owner's preference. In color, there is white, black, blue, gray, silver, brown, cafe-au-lait, apricot, and cream. Poodles do not shed hair like other breeds but they should be brushed and combed every day, or as often as possible, to remove the dead hair before it

144 has a chance to mat.

Schipperke

Height: 12–14 inches (30–36 cm); weight: 18 pounds (8 kg) maximum.

The Schipperke (pronounced *Skip-per-kee*) received its name from the Antwerp boatmen on whose craft the little dog served as a watchman. The Flemish word for boat is *schip,* so Schipperke was "little boatman." After Queen Maria Henrietta of Belgium saw a Schipperke at the Brussels show in 1885, she acquired the winning dog. This was the spark needed to start the little fellow on his career as a fashionable dog. The black Schip has a fairly wide foxlike head, narrowing at the eyes. He has a short, thick-set body. The abundant double coat is slightly harsh to the touch. It is fairly short on the body, but longer around the neck, forming a ruff. The small, dark, oval eyes have a questioning expression, sharp and lively, not mean or wild. The Schip is active, agile, indefatigable, continually occupied with what is going on around him. He is careful of things that are given him to guard, kind with children, and he quickly learns the ways of the household. The Schip is suspicious of strangers and he is slow to make friends. However, to his owners he is loyal and devoted. Rather high strung, the little black dog must be treated with kindness and understanding as well as firmness.

146

▲ *Schipperke puppy*

Tibetan Terrier

Height: 14–16 inches (36–41 cm); weight: 18–30 pounds (8–14 kg).

The Tibetan Terrier, an ancient breed, is said to have originated in the Lost Valley in Tibet. So inaccessible was Lost Valley that the occasional visitor was given a dog to safeguard the trip to the outside world. So it was that Dr. A.H.R. Greig received a dog from a Tibetan patient. In India, and later in England, the physician bred and raised a number of Tibetan Terriers. The Tibetans may be any color, including white. Their double coat covers a compact and powerful body. The medium-length feathered tail, set on fairly high, is carried in a gay curl over the back. Frequently, there is a kink near the tip. To protect the animal from the rough terrain during the Tibetan winters, the dog has large round feet, heavily furnished with hair between the toes and pads. In general appearance, he somewhat resembles a miniature Old English Sheepdog. The terrier part of the name is a misnomer, since the breed does not burrow into the ground nor does it have a terrier disposition. The Tibetan is quiet about the house and is an excellent watchdog, with a unique bark that starts on a low note and rises like a siren.

▲ *Australian Kelpie directed by "eye" to control sheep* ▼ *Border Collie*

7

Miscellaneous

Although there are several hundred breeds registered with canine organizations around the world, we have stressed those principally in the American Kennel Club stud book, which is more exclusive than the Social Register. Starting in 1878 with just 10 breeds, it was not too difficult to be listed in those early years. But from 1945, when the Black and Tan Coonhound made the grade, until 1977, when the Bearded Collie became the 122nd breed eligible to be shown, only eight other breeds had been accepted. A stepping stone for a listing is the miscellaneous class. This class has been provided so breeds long established in their native lands may have an opportunity to compete against each other. When the A.K.C. feels a breed has expanded sufficiently over a wide geographic area in the United States, it may be admitted for listing in the stud book. **149**

Australian Cattle Dog

Height: 18 inches (46 cm); weight: 33 pounds (15 kg).

This animal, also known as a Blue Cattle Dog, is one of those serious workers on which part of the Australian economy depends. They help move cattle over thousands of miles of ranch land, running in a circle around the herd to keep the animals together and nipping at the heels of the strays to head them off. He is said to be a cross of Collie, Kelpie, and Dingo, which is Australia's wild dog. Of considerable substance, the Cattle Dog has a straight, moderately short coat. The color is distinctive, the body being blue mottled, with or without black markings. The V-shaped head may be blue or marked with black and tan. There is tan on the forelegs midway, running up to the front of the chest and throat.

Australian Kelpie

Height: 17–20 inches (43–51 cm); weight: 25–30 pounds (11–14 kg).

The Kelpie, or Barb, tends sheep, rounding them up and driving them to their shed. Directed by sign and whistle, his sight, scent, and hearing are remarkable. He can read hand signals at considerable distances. Descended from the Border Collie and Dingo, the Kelpie is rather lightly made. He has a foxlike head and long, bushy tail. The coat is short, straight,

Australian Red Kelpie ▲ *Border Collie* ▶

and dense, its texture hard. Colors vary—black, red, black and tan, red and tan, fawn, chocolate, or smoke blue. A keen, alert expression is characteristic. The ears, set wide apart, are carried erect and inclined outward.

Border Collie

Height: 19–21 inches (48–53 cm); weight: 30–50 pounds (14–23 kg).

This breed has been known in Britain for more than four centuries. The sheepherder never worried much about appear-pearance or conformation of his dogs—his concern was to have an intelligent animal who could handle sheep. The Border usually is black, although sometimes gray or blue merle. He has white around the neck, chest, face, feet, and tail tip. The coat may be wavy, slightly curly, and of varying length. It is very dense and especially heavy on the neck, where the mane is abundant. The forelegs are shorter than the hind legs, so the dog's stance looks as if he was bracing himself to hold back his flock. Another hallmark is the bold and alert head carriage, indicating that he means business. His head is the old-fashioned Collie type, shorter and more blunt in muzzle and broader in skull than the modern Collie.

Cavalier King Charles Spaniel

Height: 12–13 inches (30–33 cm); weight 13–18 pounds (6–8 kg).

This is a renovated English Toy Spaniel. Instead of the ultrashort face of the toy, Cavalier fanciers have bred back to what the breed of the 17th century had been, when these dogs had a hunting spaniel head. The Cavalier now is an active, free-mover, sporting in character. He has a long, silky, soft coat. Feathering on the feet is a feature of the breed. In color, they are white with chestnut red markings, tricolor (white, black, and red), solid rich red, and black and tan. The large, round eyes are very dark, giving a lustrous look.

Ibizan Hound

Height: 22½–27½ inches (57–70 cm); weight: 42–52 pounds (19–24 kg).

The Ibizan, or *Podenco Ibicenco,* as it is called in Spain, is believed to be the modern survivor of the prick-eared ringtailed greyhound that lived in Egypt 5,000 years ago. The breed survived in its original form in the Ballearic Islands in the Mediterranean, above all on Ibiza, where it got its name. He has a long narrow head, the most distinguishing feature being prominent, erect ears. The Ibizan has a short coat, which is white and red, white and lion, or solid white, red, or lion. The dog has keen hearing, and he has tremendous ability to high jump and broad jump. Hannibal is said to have taken some of these hounds with him across the Alps into Italy. A Phoenician coin, found in Ibiza, bears the dog's image.

Spinoni Italiani

Height: 23–26 inches (56–66 cm); weight: 50–75 pounds (23–24 kg).

The Spinoni is one of the rare breeds in America. This coarse-haired pointer from Italy is popular with sportsmen in his native land, where he has proved a good all-purpose dog, excelling as an upland hunter and as a waterfowl retriever. The head is rather large and long, the ears are that of a hound, dropped and hanging close to the cheeks. He is white, white with orange markings, white with liver markings. Long, stiff hair forms the eyebrows, and he has a mustache and beard. The Spinoni is an affectionate, gentle dog, who loves **152** everyone, particularly children.

Miniature Bull Terrier

Height: 14 inches (36 cm) maximum; weight: 20 pounds (9 kg) maximum.

The Miniature, a small version of the Bull Terrier, is a sturdy little dog noted for his tenacity and courage. Muscular, active, and full of fire, he still is good tempered and amenable to discipline.

Tibetan Spaniel

Height: 9–10 inches (23–25 cm); weight: 9–15 pounds (4–7 kg).

This little dog has a long history in Tibet, where he had been so prized that in the early 18th century, several were sent annually as tribute to the Chinese emperors. He arrived in the United States only in 1966. The head is small in proportion to the body but it is proudly carried, giving an impression of quality. The spaniel is slightly longer in body than tall. His richly plumed tail is curled over the back. The double coat is silky in texture, and all colors are acceptable. This is a hardy dog, some living to be 23 or 24 years old. The coat needs a weekly brushing. They do not make good kennel dogs as they crave human companionship. **153**

▲ *Tibetan Spaniel*

Glossary

Balanced—Symmetrically proportioned as a whole.

Bat ears—Erect ears, broad at base and rounded at top.

Bay—The sound a hunting hound makes when trailing or running a quarry.

Belton—A coat coloration consisting of a white background, heavily flecked with darker hairs. If flecked with blue-gray it is called blue belton, if orange flecked it is orange belton.

Bench show—A show where benches are provided for the dogs when they are not in the ring. The benches are raised platforms, divided into stalls. The dogs are required to remain on them all day so visitors may see the various breeds.

Blaze—White mark running up the middle of the face and between the eyes.

Bloat—Excessive gas in stomach causing acute gastric dilation.

Blue—Coat color with a bluish or smoky cast.

Blue merle—Blue and gray mixed with black; marbled.

Brindle—Black stripes on a lighter color coat; black hairs mixed with other colors.

Clip—A method of trimming the coat.

Cobby—Compact in body build.

Conformation—Structure and form according to the breed standards.

Coursing—Sport in which greyhounds pursue hares.

Cropped ears—Trimmed in puppyhood to stand erect and pointed.

Dapple—Mottled markings of different colors, no one predominating.

Docked tail—Shortened by cutting the tail in puppyhood.

Dome—Convexity of skull.

Dropped ears—Ears hanging flat and close to the cheeks.

Dual purpose—Suited for both working and showing.

Fancier—One particularly interested in breeding and showing purebred dogs.

Feathering—Long silky fringe of hair on legs, ears, tail, or body.

Field—Terrain for hunting.

Field trial—A competition for dogs to test their ability and style in finding or retrieving game.

Furnishings—Thick, fringed, or long portions of the coat, especially on legs, face, and ears.

Gait—Manner of walking, trotting, or running.

Giving tongue—Hound's voice, cry, or note when running a trail.

Grizzle—Bluish gray color; mixture of black and white hair.

Harlequin—A white dog with torn patches irregularly and well distributed over entire body.

Height—Vertical measurement from highest point of shoulders to ground.

Hip dysplasia—Hereditary deformity of the hip joint.

Hound color—White, tan, and black.

Kennel—Enclosure where dogs are housed; establishment of a breeder.

Mane—Thick hair around the neck and throat.

Mask—Dark marking on muzzle, sometimes extending over eyes.

Muzzle—Part of head from eyes to nose; foreface.

Nose—Ability of a dog to scent.

Pack—Group of hounds that regularly hunt together.

Pads—Soles of paws.

Parti-color—Two or more clear and distinct colors in a coat.

Plucking—Method of pulling out loose hair by hand.

Plume—A tail with profuse hair.

Point—Immovable stance of the hunting dog to indicate the presence and position of game.

Prick ears—Erect and usually pointed.

Purebred—Having ancestors of the same breed since its recognition.

Recognition—Acceptance of a breed on the register of a national or international canine organization.

Roach back—Convex curvature of the back.

Ruff—Thick long hair around the neck.

Sable—Dark brown shaded with black hairs.

Saddle—Saddle-shaped black marking over back and shoulders.

Standard—Description of an ideal dog of a particular breed established by national canine organizations to serve as a guide for judging at shows.

Steady—A hunting dog who remains motionless after the birds he has found have been flushed and a shot fired.

Substance—Bone structure, physical solidity.

Ticked—Small splashes of colored hairs on a basically white coat.

Topknot—A clump of long hair on top of the head.

Topline—The line along the dog's back in profile.

Type—Essential characteristics distinguishing a breed.

Wheaten—Pale yellow or fawn color.

Wild boar—Tan undercoat with black or grizzle overlay.

Wrinkle—Loosely folded skin on sides of face or forehead.

Dog Organizations

The American Kennel Club is the dominant force of the dog world in the United States, registering canines, keeping a stud book, making the rules for shows and trials, and licensing judges and professional handlers. The United Kennel Club registers some breeds not recognized by the A.K.C. and conducts bench shows, field trials, coonhound night hunts, and water races. The Federation Cynologique Internationale is the ruling body for world dogdom.

United States

American Kennel Club
51 Madison Avenue
New York, New York 10010

American Field
222 West Adams Street
Chicago, Illinois 60606

American Rescue Dog
10714 Royal Springs Drive
Dallas, Texas 75229

American Sighthound Field
 Association
9590 Trenton Way
Stockton, California 95205

American Working Terrier
R.D. 1, Penn Yan, New York
 14527

International Sled Dog
 Racing Association
460 South 43 Street
Boulder, Colorado 80303

North American Working
 Dogs of America
1677 North Alisar Avenue
Monterey Park, California
 91754

United Kennel Club
321 West Cedar Street
Kalamazoo, Michigan 49006

United States Professional
Dog Trainers Association
4282 Austin Boulevard
Island Park, New York 11558

Working Dogs of America
1164 Wall Road
Webster, New York 14580

International

Federation Cynologique
 Internationale (F.C.I.)
14, Rue Leopold II
6530 Thuin, Belgium

Argentina

Kennel Club Argentino
Florida, 671
Buenos Aires

Australia

Australian Nat. Kennel Council
Royal Show Grounds
Ascot Vale 3002, Victoria

Austria

Oesterreichischer
 Kynologenverband
Karl Schweighofergasse, 3
A-1070, Vienna

Belgium

Union Cynologique St. Hubert
Avenue de l'Armee, 25,
 B-1040 Brussels

Bermuda

Bermuda Kennel Club
P.O. 1455, Hamilton

Brazil

Brazil Kennel Club
Caixa Post. 1468, Rio de
 Janeiro

Canada

Canadian Kennel Club
2150 Bloor Street West
Toronto, Ontario
M6S 4V7

Caribbean

Caribbean Kennel Club
P.O. 737, Port of Spain
Trinidad

Chile

Kennel Club of Chile
Casilla 1704, Valparaiso

Colombia

Club Canino Colombiano
Carrera 7a, 84-61
Apartamento 101, Bogota

Czechoslovakia

Federal. Vybor Mysliveckych
Svazu v CSSR
Husova 7 115 25, Praha 1

Denmark

Dansk Kennelklub
Parkvej 1, Jersie Strand
DK 2680 Solrod Strand

Dominican Republic

Asociacion Canina
 Dominicana
Apartado 420
Santo Domingo

Ecuador

Asociacion Canina
 Ecuatoriana
Casilla Postal 533
Quito

Finland

Suomen Kennelliitto
Finska Kennelklubben
Bulevardi 14, 00120
 Helsinki 12

France
Societe Central Canine
215 Rue St. Denis
75083 Paris Cedex 02

Germany West
Verband fuer die Deutsche
Hundewesen
Schwanenstrasse 30
D-46, Dortmund

Great Britain
The Kennel Club
1 Clarges St., Piccadilly
London, W1Y 8AB

Greece
Ellinikos Kynologikos
Organismos
Rue Irodotou 24A, Athens

Hungary
Magyar Ebtenyesztok
Orszagos Egyesulete
H-1114 Fadrusz Utca 11/8
Budapest

India
Kennel Club of India
Coonoor—1
Dist: Nilgiris, S.

Ireland
Irish Kennel Club
Fottrell House
23 Earlsfort Terrace
Dublin 2

Israel
Israel Kennel Club
P.O. Box 33055, Tel Aviv

Italy
Ente Nazionale della Cinofilia
Viale Premuda 21
1-20129, Milan

Japan
Japan Dog Federation
9-8, 3-chome, Uchi-Kanda
Chiyodaku, Tokyo

Luxembourg
Union Cynologique du
Grand-Duche de
Luxembourg
Rue J.P. Huberty 42

Mexico
Asociacion Canofila Mexicana
Zacatecas 229-Desp. 318
Mexico 7, D.F.

Monaco
Societe Canine de Monaco
Palais des Congres
Ave. d'Ostende, Monte Carlo

Morocco
Societe Central Canine
Marocaine
Boite Postale 78, Rabat

Netherlands
Raad van Beheer op
Kynologisch
Gebied in Nederland
Emmalaan 16, NL,
Amsterdam 2

New Zealand
New Zealand Kennel Club
P.O. Box 19101, Wellington 1

Norway
Norsk Kennel Club
Postboks 6598—Rodelokka
Teglverset 8, Oslo 5

Panama
Club Canino de Panama
Apartado 3273
Panama 3

Paraguay
Paraguay Kennel Club
Estrella 851, Oficina 3
Casilla de Correo 644,
Asuncion

Peru
Kennel Club Peruano
Jiron de la Union 264 5to
Piso Of. 503, Lima

Poland
Zwiazek Kynologiczny
v Polsce
Nowy-Swiat 35, Warsaw

Portugal
Clube Portugues de
Canicultura
Praca D.Joao Da Camara 4
Lisbon 2

Puerto Rico
Puerto Rican Kennel Club
P.O. Box 4876
San Juan, P.R. 00905

South Africa
Kennel Union of Southern
Africa
P.O. Box 562, Cape Town

Soviet Union
State Kennels
(Alexander Pavlovich
Mazover)
House #120, Block 1, Flat 109
Leningradskoye Shossee
Moscow 125445

Spain
Real Sociedad Central de
Fomento de la Razas
Caninas
Los Madrazo 20, Madrid 14

Sweden
Svenska Kennelklubben
Box 1308, S-11183,
Stockholm

Switzerland
Societe Cynologique Suisse
Case Postale 2307, Ch-3001
Berne 1 Facher

Uruguay
Kennel Club Uruguayo
Av. Uruguay 864
Montevideo

Venezuela
Federacion Canina de
Venezuela
1064 Apartado, Caracas

Index

159

Walter R. Fletcher, a staff member of the New York *Times* for 50 years, is known on five continents for his dog writing. During his career he has covered more than 1,500 dog shows, in addition to writing dog columns twice weekly. A native New Yorker, he is a graduate of City College. He has won numerous prizes, including a citation from the Institute for Human-Animal Relationship "for outstanding humanitarian endeavors and accomplishments," two awards from the New York *Times* publisher, and 24 from the Dog Writers' Association of America. Fletcher is an honorary member of the Austrian, Brazil, and Portuguese kennel clubs, the Owner-Handler Association of America, the International Dog Society of Japan, several kennel clubs in the U.S.A., and Eskimo Dog Society of Northwest Territories.